For Sandi:
None of this would be possible without you.
I am grateful beyond words.
YTMBA!

"Life is difficult."
—*M. Scott Peck*

"Life is tough . . . but it's much tougher if you're stupid."
—*John Wayne*

CONTENTS

CHAPTER 1

THE DREADED DUMB TAX

"It is not supposed to be easy. Anyone who finds it easy is stupid."
—*Charlie Munger, Vice Chairman of Berkshire Hathaway*

Smart people do dumb things.

Here's the proof: How much money would you have right now if I gave you the ability to unwind any three financial decisions you have ever made? Write that number down . . . seriously.

Over the last thirty years of mentoring, coaching, advising, and teaching business owners, I have asked this simple question to tens of thousands of entrepreneurs, business owners, and CEOs. I have yet to have anyone tell me her wealth or income would be unchanged.

Chances are the erroneous assumptions you made that caused these financial mistakes were obvious with the passage of time. The problem is that by the time you woke up and smelled the coffee, the decision had been made and the loss incurred.

We have all paid "dumb tax"; mine is in the tens of millions.

I am a smart man, but not as smart as I think I am. I am an expert at business and investing, yet I have been bankrupt. The intergalactically dumb decisions and assumptions that caused this financial disaster were not a result of an inadequate IQ but rather an unwillingness to use it.

Thinking is critical to sustainable success in business; said another way, business is an intellectual sport.

The bulk of my problems are a result of indigestion and greed, not starvation. Had I been more thoughtful (and less emotionally impulsive) in the initial decision-making process, I would have made far fewer bad choices and, as a result, my wealth would be many multiples of what it is today . . . and so would yours.

Years ago, after suffering a humiliatingly large dumb tax, it dawned on me that I have a seemingly unlimited ability to hit unforced errors and sabotage my business and financial success.

Here is my startling, yet obvious conclusion and the premise for this book: It turns out that the key to getting rich (and staying that way) is to avoid doing stupid things. I don't need to do more smart things. I just need to do fewer dumb things. I need to avoid making emotional decisions and swinging at bad pitches. I need to think!

Here it is on a bumper sticker: All my problems started out as a good idea and all those "good" ideas were emotionally justifiable at the time. Not only that, my current financial condition represents my very best "thinking." Yours does too.

I have yet to wake up in the morning and say to myself, "Okay, Keith, today is the day you are going to permanently screw up the rest of your life. Today you will do some things that will have major catastrophic consequences for decades to come. Today is the day you will not use your best ideas or even your second-best ideas. Today is the day you will only use your third-best ideas!" When you stop to think about it, what sabotages our dreams and causes most of our problems (and ensuing dumb tax) is our excessive optimism and emotional belief in magic pills, secret formulas, and financial tooth fairies. (All balloons look good when they are filled with hot air.) Dumb!

We make it harder than it needs to be. We gravitate toward impulsive, glandular decisions instead of thoughtful, rational ones.

As John Maynard Keynes astutely said, "Most people, when confronted with a choice of changing their thoughts or proving there is no need to change, get busy on the proof."

Here it is on a bumper sticker: Emotions and intellect work inversely. When emotions go up, intellect goes down. Optimism is a deadly emotion in the business world. Warren Buffett said it best: "Optimism is the enemy of the rational investor."

In other words, I need fewer "good ideas." Well . . . that's not exactly true. I need fewer good ideas that I jump out of my chair and execute without weighing the alternatives and thinking about what could go wrong (the 2nd-, 3rd-, and 4th-order consequences) and whether or not those consequences are acceptable.

More often than not, critically thinking about what could go wrong and doing the work to mitigate those risks before taking action is abandoned in favor of comfort zones, the path of least resistance, and speed (instant gratification).

Most of us have heard of, own, and in some cases actually read a book that was first published almost eighty years ago. With more than 70 million copies sold since its original publication in 1937, this international best seller is considered to be the bible for business success. The name of Napoleon Hill's book is *Think and Grow Rich*. It isn't "Use Your Gut and Grow Rich" or "Sit in a Dark Room, Om, and Visualize a Sack Full of Money Dropping on Your Head and Grow Rich" or "Do What You Love and Grow Rich." It's not about touching yourself, closing your eyes, or relying on fantasy economics (which are only effective in fantasies). And it's certainly not a "Secret." It's THINK! (There are no secrets . . . just stuff you haven't learned yet.)

My outcome for this book is that it will add to your tool belt, knowledge, and insights to support you in being thoughtful about your decisions and decision-making process prior to taking action. You will run your business more effectively, make more money, and dramatically increase the likelihood of keeping that money if you adopt the discipline of Thinking Time.

CHAPTER 2

THE DISCIPLINE OF THINKING TIME

"I insist on a lot of time being spent thinking, almost every day, to just sit and think. That is very uncommon in American business. I read and think. So I do more reading and thinking, and make less impulse decisions than most people in business. I do it because I like this kind of life."
—*Warren Buffett*

The idea of writing a book about Thinking Time (which I am hoping was not my 3rd-best idea) has been in the making for decades. It started over twenty-five years ago (shortly after I paid a gigantic dumb tax), when I began tracking and recording the critical skills, tools, and insights I learned the hard way and which I have found are necessary to be sustainably successful. In the process, I have developed several core beliefs that have molded my thinking, actions, and results. Here are the critical few that are relevant for this book:

- **There is no such thing as a natural business owner.** Successful business owners and entrepreneurs are not born with an innate set of skills that produce business excellence and success. <u>Great business owners work hard, practice, study, test, think, correct, and</u>

practice some more. None are infallible or perfect, but all are committed to excellence and mastery of the game.

- **Attempting to win the game of business by trial and error is about the stupidest way to learn anything.** Trial and error is a "Pin the Tail on the Donkey" strategy that is painful, slow, and expensive, and it rarely succeeds. If I wanted to call you on the phone, I could Google your number, or I could start randomly dialing numbers in the hope I would one day stumble onto the right combination. By then, of course, I would have forgotten what I wanted to talk to you about.

- **Running the wrong direction enthusiastically is stupid.** It does no good to practice the wrong thing. Practice does not make perfect. Practice makes permanent. To excel, we need a coach or an advisor to watch our swing and provide candid advice about what we are doing wrong and how we can do better.

- **If you want to do better, you must get better.** People do not do better because they *want to do better*; they do better because they *get better*. You cannot achieve a new outcome without learning something new and practicing what you learned (probably outside your comfort zone). A commitment to mastery (improving) is essential for excellence.

- **The people with the best life have the best choices.** People with a lousy life have lousy choices. If I want to improve my life, I need to create better choices.

Here it is on a bumper sticker: You will pay the dumb tax if you ignore these principles or you will pay to fix the problem. Either way, you are writing a check. One happens to be far smaller than the other.

The Road Less Stupid is designed to accomplish two primary objectives:

1. Provide a structure/process/skill set to enable you to create a successful Thinking Time ritual that, if applied, will result in a significantly reduced dumb tax. The Thinking Time process I have

developed and used over the last twenty-five years is described in the first couple of chapters.

2. Suggest a series of possible Thinking Time topics and questions you can use to spark your thinking, grow your business, make more money, and ultimately avoid doing something stupid.

The Road Less Stupid is a direct result not only of my experience of owning and running businesses but also, more importantly, from working closely with founders, CEOs and business owners in an intimate Board of Directors environment. The topics I am writing about are the most common issues I have encountered with our clients and Board members, regardless of their company's size or industry. I think you will find the majority of these topics, lessons, and questions are relevant to you as well.

The book is organized into short, stand-alone chapters and designed to be consumed in a nonlinear way. Your understanding of each chapter is not contingent on having read the prior chapters. Open this book to any chapter, start reading, and you will get my drift fairly quickly.

Most chapters will require less than five to ten minutes to read, but the insights you will get from your Thinking Time sessions (which I explain in the chapter "Thinking Time: The Process") will change the way you run your business and do your job. Use my Thinking Time questions as a springboard for either creating additional questions or for your actual Thinking Time session. If your business is anything like mine, revisiting a question in future Thinking Time sessions is a particularly good idea. Things tend to change at an astonishing pace; yesterday's answers rarely solve tomorrow's problems. (See the chapter "The Only Constant in Business Is . . ." if you have any doubt.)

Some chapters have an intimidating number of possible Thinking Time questions. I left all of them in each chapter so that you could have a wide range to choose from. You do not need to address each and every one; just find the high-value questions on a topic and work on those. A few are better than none.

Sometimes, I have used the same question in multiple chapters. I don't mind repeating a question if it adds value to the current Thinking

Time topic. Any of the proposed questions will help you get optics (insights) on areas in your business that need prioritization and work.

This is a business book for business readers, meant to educate rather than to entertain. Wrestling with and candidly answering my suggested questions in your Thinking Time sessions will enable you to minimize taking irrational risks and making stupid decisions (which inevitably results in an unnecessary dumb tax) and to maximize creating more robust choices and business success.

CHAPTER 3

THE 5 CORE DISCIPLINES OF THINKING

Over the last twenty-five years or so, I have practiced "Thinking Time," which is a thirty- to forty-five-minute session of uninterrupted concentration. I start by preparing a high-value question before the actual session begins. The better the question, the more insightful and robust the answers and possibilities created.

My questions are designed to help me think about a problem or situation where I am uncertain (or too certain), stuck, or have been unrealistic in my thinking, which is usually a sign that I am about to do something stupid. As the famous economist Peter Bernstein said, "The riskiest moment is when you think you are right."

While I have created hundreds of Thinking Time questions over the years, they usually revolve around five core disciplines:

1. **Find the Unasked Question**—Create a question that will result in clarity and generate better choices.

2. **Separate the Problem from the Symptom**—Identify the real obstacle that is blocking my progress.

3. **Check Assumptions**—Differentiate the facts from the story I am spinning.

4. **Consider 2nd-Order Consequences**—Clarify the risks and the possibility/cost of being wrong.

5. **Create the Machine**—Create the executable plan and identify the resources (people and money) required to solve the real (core) problem and make forward progress.

These Thinking Time disciplines are interdependent and must all be mastered to minimize the likelihood of stupid.

CORE DISCIPLINE #1— FIND THE UNASKED QUESTION

When we get stuck, we tend to think the reason is because we don't have the right answer. My experience is that finding the "right" answer is rarely the problem. <u>What keeps us stuck are inferior questions that produce tactical or unattractive choices.</u>

A problem is simply an unanswered question. (Sadly, most unanswered questions remain unanswered because the question was never asked.) If there are no possible solutions or available improvements to the situation, it is not a problem but rather a predicament. A predicament is a state of environment—for instance, the price of oil, being sixty-four years old, or a tornado. Nothing you can do about it. I can't change the environment, only how I will play the game given the environment I'm in.

Framing the problem as a statement is always a mistake. A statement tricks your brain into thinking this situation is a fact and not a question that needs a solution. "I am poor" provides no insight on how to remedy this situation . . . and neither does "Why am I poor?"

I have a couple of tricks I use to help expand the number of possible choices. One is to <u>frame the problem as a "How might I . . . so that I can . . ." question.</u> "How might I generate an additional $20,000/month in profits so that we can afford to invest in a new building and double our capacity?" is a lot better than "Our profits suck" or "Why do our profits suck?" I also think about "How did it get this way? Why does it stay this way? How can I improve the way it looks?"

One added benefit of the "How might I . . . so that I can . . ." question is that it helps me think about what needs to be broken vs. what needs to be fixed. A common mistake we make as business owners is to assume that the problem identified is a situation that needs to be repaired, duct-taped, or mended. My experience is that often the machine I currently have is not the machine I need. (In "Correcting the Business Model" I explain this in greater depth.) Putting wings on a bicycle does not make it airworthy.

A great question always has three common characteristics:

1. It provides insight on what the actual problem is that needs to be addressed.

2. It simplifies the problem and makes it solvable.

3. It expands the number of possibilities available to solve the problem or improve the situation.

Here it is on a bumper sticker: Having the right answer is smart. Having the right question is genius. Or, as Peter Drucker said, "Most serious mistakes are not being made as a result of wrong answers. The truly dangerous thing is asking the wrong question."

All problems are solvable (or at a minimum can be addressed so that we improve our situation). Our job as business owners and leadership teams is to get clarity on the right question to ask before we pull the trigger. We would all have better answers and more choices if we invested the time to design better questions and then actually allocated some Thinking Time to consider them.

CORE DISCIPLINE #2—
SEPARATE THE PROBLEM FROM THE SYMPTOM

If I asked you to write down on a piece of paper one of the three biggest problems you are currently facing in your business, you could immediately start your list. Your grievances might include not enough sales, not enough customers, not enough people know about you, not enough cash, not enough profits, can't find qualified employees, can't keep good staff, can't afford A-player candidates (the list can get pretty long).

Most people, when asked to pinpoint their biggest problem, erroneously identify their problems as the gap between where they are and where they would like to be. For proof, check the answer you were about to write down. What you identified as the *problem* is actually a description of the *gap*. The gap is not your core underlying problem; it's the *symptom*. The symptom is what indicates something is wrong, but it does not shed any light on what is causing it to show up.

Clearly, something is wrong in each of the examples listed above. Although painful, not one of these examples is the *real* root problem. We can spend hours fretting about and describing the "problem" (in glorious detail) yet remain frustrated by a lack of clear solutions or better choices. In fact, the better I get at telling the story, the deeper the trance (and invariably a victim mentality). Your story is your story. Retelling your story does not help you change it. Nor does it help you discover a solution.

We mistakenly believe we know what our problems are because we can identify the places we don't have what we want (the gap or symptoms). The core problem is never the obvious gap comparison between what "is" (Point A) and what "ought" (Point B).

The key to defining the root problem is discovering the *obstacle* (it resides in the gap) that is impeding your progress from here to there. It is the obstacle that is the problem, not the dissatisfaction with your current circumstances!

There are two fundamental difficulties with a misdiagnosis of the root problem (or mislabeling the symptom as the obstacle):

1. The questions you ask and the solutions you find are usually tactical.

2. The machine that gets built to solve the perceived "problem" (which is really just the symptom) is a machine for the problem that isn't. When machines are constructed and deployed that do not address the root problem (obstacle), resources are wasted and there is zero sustainable forward progress toward the desired

outcome. This one sentence explains why most plans do not succeed: The machine that gets built addresses only the obvious symptom and does not solve the core problem or overcome the obstacle that is in the way. Building a machine for the problem that isn't and expecting forward progress is delusional.

Suppose I ask the question "How can I get in shape and lose some weight?" The observable symptom is poor health or clothes that don't fit. We erroneously label this symptom as the root problem. It's not. Then we compound the mistake by asking what we should do about it, which immediately throws our thinking into a tactical mode. Without clarity on the root problem, we make the mistake of asking "What should I do next?" instead of getting crystal clear about "*This* is the problem I want to solve." Our tendency is to search for obvious answers and tactical solutions to alleviate the discomfort of the symptom.

Based on this misdiagnosis and tactical question of what to *do* about the symptom, our thinking lurches to whether we should buy a jump rope, Oprah's new diet book, or a treadmill? Should we join a gym or buy those new Nike CrossFit trainers? The reality is the reason we weigh too much has zero to do with the jump rope or the gym . . . Bad questions beget wrong answers. Said another way: Tactical questions always produce tactical answers!

How do I know so much about this "get in shape" issue? I have an attic full of virtually unused exercise equipment. I purchased these Stairmasters and Peloton indoor exercise bikes in the mistaken belief that if I just owned the right gear, I could get in shape. Dumb!

I misdiagnosed the problem, asked the wrong questions, got tactical answers, and therefore built a machine for the problem that isn't . . . And I didn't get my outcome of getting into shape.

Diet books and elliptical trainers are tactical answers and have nothing to do with understanding or addressing the core problem that is sabotaging my fitness. I could own a dozen of them and still not have pants that fit.

Here is an example most of us have faced in our businesses. We notice that revenues are stagnant or not growing fast enough. In reality, inadequate sales are a symptom of something else. Depending on how you label and define what that something else is, you will build a machine to fix whatever you identify as the "problem." (If you miss on the problem, your solution is a waste of time and money.)

The question we typically ask when confronted with weak sales is: "What marketing initiative should we start, or how many new salespeople should we hire, or which SEO expert should we retain to secure a page-one Google ranking?" (All tactical, not strategic.)

In reality, your sales not being high enough is NOT the problem. Inadequate sales are the symptom of something else. Without clarity on your business's core underlying problem, you will be tempted to snag the closest consultant and buy her recommended solution (machine) to improve sales.

Suppose you spent forty-five minutes really thinking about the real obstacle that is preventing higher revenues. You might create a list that contains some of the following problems:

Customers not buying enough	Lack of referrals
Not enough customers	Lack of repeat business
Market is competitive	Lack of differentiation
Not enough prospects	Lack of competitive advantage
No clarity on the target market	Poor messaging
Poor lead conversion %	Not priced competitively
Weak salespeople	Weak brand . . . No promise
Inadequate sales leads	Wrong messaging channel

All the above (and hundreds of others) are possible reasons (causes) for sales being lower than planned, and each of these causes would require a completely different solution (machine). With a couple of possible exceptions, this partial list of issues does not get addressed by initiating a social media strategy or hiring more salespeople, yet any of the items on this list could be a gingerbread crumb for why sales are not as robust as desired.

And, for each of these possible "reasons/causes" there are probably subcategories of additional distinctions that might be contributing to each of these "problems." Each of the items on this list could be drilled for additional clarity about the underlying obstacle. For example, a lack of repeat business might be the reason revenues are not higher, so this presents an opportunity to ask additional questions: "Why is our repeat business not at 88%? If we ran our business so every customer would say, 'I would have to be crazy to do business with someone else,' would this solve (or help close the gap) for our revenue problem?"

Describing the problem as "sales not high enough" leads to a burst of activity that rarely solves the real problem (if it does, we got lucky), but we feel good because we are "doing something." Confusing activity with productivity is a major saboteur of business success. Just because you're sweating doesn't mean it's working.

The three most fundamental questions to ask to help get clarity about the root problem/obstacle are:

1. What are the possible reasons I am noticing this symptom?

2. What isn't happening that, if it did happen, would cause the perceived gap (symptoms) to either narrow or disappear?

3. What is happening that, if it stopped happening, would cause the perceived gap (symptoms) to narrow or disappear?

These three questions also go to the heart of Core Discipline #1— Find the Unasked Question, which I talked about above. The danger is this: If we misdiagnose or mislabel the problem, we will gravitate toward designing solutions and building machines for the symptoms (aka "the problem that isn't") and this is a prescription for frustration and failure.

The machine we create and build should always help us overcome the *obstacle* that is blocking our forward progress and momentum, not just alleviate the pain of the symptom. Find the drip, fix the leak.

Remember all those elliptical trainers in my attic? All were "machines" for the problem that isn't. The symptom was, I weighed too much. The real problem was a lack of consistent discipline, consistent diet, AND consistent exercise. As my trainer continues to tell me, "Keith, you can't out-exercise a bad diet." Smart dude!

Separating the "problem that is" from the "symptom we see" is no easy task. It often requires peer input, brutal honesty, and penetrating questions. Frankly, the process of problem identification is the most difficult part of the Thinking Time process. It's why there is so much value in having a Board of Directors (You'll learn much more about their value in "Advice from the Chairman of the Board.")

Sustainable forward progress (aka "Kicking the Can") is only possible by identifying

- exactly where I am (Point A);
- exactly where the can is;
- exactly where the goal line is in relation to me and the can (Point B); and
- then overcoming the specific obstacle preventing the can from crossing the goal line.

Messing up any one of these four will seriously impair your ability to achieve the outcomes you are striving for.

Here it is on a bumper sticker: Few things are worse than running the wrong direction enthusiastically. Misdiagnosing the problem or working on the wrong priorities results in a dumb tax!

CORE DISCIPLINE #3—CHECK ASSUMPTIONS

All those good ideas that turned out bad have one thing in common: unexamined assumptions, which usually take the form of a really great story. Thinking Time gives me an opportunity to test the validity of the assumptions I am making (or the story I am telling). The key to checking assumptions is to look for where I have substituted an opinion for a fact. Consider, for example:

- Most people assumed that computers would do away with paper. (We use more paper today than ever before.)

- Kodak assumed digital photography would never catch on. (They invented it, didn't see the potential, and doubled down on film. Bankruptcy is a bitter pill.)

- The Swiss invented the battery-powered watch. (They assumed it was a bad idea, and failed to protect the idea with a patent. The Japanese are grateful for the arrogance of the Swiss.)

- Myspace thought the key to global domination was a first-mover advantage. (Facebook proved that was a stupid assumption.)

One of my most frequent Thinking Time questions is: "What Don't I See?" I like it so much that it is on prominent display in my office, including as a screen saver on my computer. This question is powerful because what I don't see is what costs me money.

What none of us see are the assumptions we make about the problem we have, the solution we create, or the opportunity in front of us. The reality is that virtually all my dumb tax could have been avoided if I had just questioned a couple of obvious assumptions prior to pulling the trigger.

Looking back with the benefit of 20/20 hindsight, it is clear that many of my original assumptions were highly unrealistic, overly optimistic, or just plain stupid . . . and they all went unquestioned at the time.

An assumption I used to make quite frequently was "lottery investing" (small investment, high probability of failure, but astronomical returns if lucky). My friends and business associates that required third-party capital would frequently present me their deals. Typically, I would throw small amounts of money at these very high-risk opportunities in the misguided belief (assumption) that the amount of money being risked was easily digestible in the event of a loss . . . but, if it worked, was easily justifiable as genius. Then I heard a really intriguing story about Warren Buffett playing golf.

Warren (who admits he is a lousy golfer) was on a Par 3 hole with his three companions (one of whom was rumored to be his best friend, Bill Gates). As Warren prepared to tee off, one of his playing partners suggested a wager. "Warren, I'll bet $20 you don't hit a hole in one." Warren replied, "What odds will you give me?" His partner said, "1,000 to 1," which meant that if Warren didn't hit a hole in one, he would owe $20, but if he did make the shot, he would receive $20,000.

Warren immediately responded, "No bet . . . Bad odds." His golfing companion was stunned. "Warren, it's $20! Last year you made $5.3 billion. You can afford it, man!"

I'll never forget Buffett's reply. "If I stood here and hit a thousand golf balls, the likelihood that any of them would go in the hole is very remote. Maybe if I hit 10,000 golf balls I might get lucky and one would go in; but, you are not offering 10,000 to 1 odds. I know it's a small amount of money and that I could easily afford it, but it's bad odds. Stupid in small things, stupid in big things."

I am confident that your experience mirrors mine. We would both be better off if we spent some quality Thinking Time differentiating the facts from our emotions and fantasies.

CORE DISCIPLINE #4—
CONSIDER THE 2ND-ORDER CONSEQUENCES

Nothing wrong with eating that Krispy Kreme or investing in your brother-in-law's "athletic sock that doubles as a pot holder" start-up business if you have thought through the possible 2nd-order consequences. I use the following three questions (which I call the Power of 3) as one of my litmus tests to help me think before I act:

- **What is the upside?** We are usually experts at this one.

- **What is the downside?** What could go wrong? We rarely can do this one by ourselves because we are irrationally emotional and optimistic about the thing we are deciding about.

- **Can I live with the downside?** Only the pros bother to think about this one, which is why their track record of dumb tax is so much smaller than the track record of the rest of us mortals.

("The 4 Hats of Business" and "Creating Enterprise Value" each go into more detail about these questions.)

Unexamined 2nd-order consequences is simply another way of asking you to consider the possibility of being wrong.

In a famous episode during their rule of colonial India, the British failed to consider the 2nd-order consequences or the possibility of being wrong in the snake eradication debacle. Being new to the area, the British were deathly afraid of the large number of venomous king cobras in New Delhi, so they offered a generous bounty for every dead cobra collected.

The bounty system was a fantastic success, with huge numbers of dead cobras soon turned in for the reward. As the available pool of snakes dwindled and bounties became more difficult to collect, some entrepreneurial Indians realized they could breed these snakes in captivity and thus continue to receive the bounty. Soon a large cottage industry of snake farming sprang into life. When the British became aware of this scheme, they immediately scrapped the bounty program. Naturally, the cobra farmers now had no use for the thousands of poisonous snakes they were raising, so they released them back into the wild. The 2nd-order consequence? The number of king cobras in New Delhi was twice as large as it was before this "good idea" was hatched.

Here it is on a bumper sticker: We only have a choice about the decision we are about to make, not the consequences. An important decision that does not identify the possible risks as well as the probability and costs of failure is a decision with a high likelihood of creating drama. The problem with drama is that it always costs money.

Risks don't cease to exist just because you ignore them, and neither do facts. An honest assessment of what could go wrong, the probability of it going off the rails, and the cost in the event of failure are fundamental to minimizing your dumb tax. (Spend some time in the "Not All Risks Are Created Equal" chapter to further reduce the likelihood of an avoidable dumb tax.)

Many years ago I was playing golf with Tom Kite, a leading money winner on the PGA tour at the time and now a member of the World Golf Hall of Fame.

On the 16th hole, I hit my ball deep into the woods. After searching for several minutes, we found the ball nestled against a bush. In evaluating my next shot, it was obvious my swing would be awkward and very constricted. I looked up and noticed about a three-foot gap in the trees that was in the general direction of the hole. The gap was maybe fifteen or twenty feet off the ground and probably thirty yards in front of me. As I was thinking about attempting this miracle shot, Tom was watching me very closely.

"Keith, do you know what a par is?" he asked.

"Of course," I replied. "It's the number of strokes a good player should normally require on a hole. This is a Par 4 hole."

Then he asked, "Do you know what a bogey is?" Since I play golf, this was a seemingly obvious and unnecessary question at this particular moment.

"One over par," I answered as I reached for the club I intended to use to pull off this incredible recovery shot.

"Right. Do you know what a double bogey is, Keith?"

Now I was getting a little irritated. I am trying to concentrate on my swing and hitting the ball exactly right, and Tom is over there playing twenty questions with me. I mustered some degree of calm in my voice and respectfully replied, "It is two over par, Tom."

Tom's answer has stuck with me for over twenty-five years now. "No, a double bogey is a bad shot followed by a stupid shot."

Here it is on a bumper sticker: Thinking about 2nd-order consequences minimizes the probability of a double bogey. Mistakes are inevitable, but double bogeys are usually avoidable.

I placed my original club back into the bag, selected a new club, chipped out sideways, and made a bogey—and dodged the dreaded dumb tax. Tom is a smart man! (I still wonder if I could have pulled that shot off.)

CORE DISCIPLINE #5—CREATE THE MACHINE

Thinking Time helps me get clarity on the core problem. Clarity about the desired outcome and the obstacles preventing the achievement of this outcome are critical. But a description of the destination is not a substitute for the road map, or the machine, that will get me there.

Here it is on a bumper sticker: Shoes that don't fit are not a bargain at any price. A good idea that can't be executed is a bad idea.

Ultimately, the problem gets addressed or solved as a result of a machine that will move me from Point A (where I am) to Point B (where I want to go). The expectation is that the new machine will produce an output that improves my situation, closes the gap, and moves me closer to the desired outcome. (In "The Big 8" I describe in detail the process of creating the machine.)

Building an effective machine or adapting the current machine implies actual activity, and that activity will be different from what is currently being executed.

Maybe you have discovered a new obstacle that can only be overcome with a new strategy. Maybe the change is with the business model, the distribution channel, or the marketing message/medium. Maybe the change is expanding from a local stand-alone shop to scaling a franchise or internet-based business.

Here it is on a bumper sticker: Regardless of the change, management must shift priorities if the new solution has a shot at being effective. Changes in priorities are always accompanied by changes in the allocation of resources. The vast majority of solutions (machines) fail to produce the anticipated outcomes because management is unclear about the required shifts in focus, human capital, and money.

Machines require people to operate them. When you stop to think about it, a great machine that is operated by a team of B and C players who execute inconsistently and are a poor cultural fit is a machine doomed to mediocrity or the dump. It is literally a waste of time to think about a machine and not simultaneously think about the execution and the essential resources required to operate the machine. (I devote quite a bit of time to this issue in "A CEO Should *Never* Delegate . . .")

Consistent execution requires dashboards, processes, best practices, standards, metrics, and accountability to measure the critical drivers, monitor the progress, reward the success, and coach/train the people operating it. Measurement allows you to see which improvements (or corrections) are required in the execution to enhance the outputs and thereby accelerate the progress. All execution must be monitored and corrected, but these refinements are dictated by the dashboards, scoreboards, and measurements. Measurement is THE key to sustainability and a culture of accountability.

The machine is where the "Paprika Effect" is most likely to arise, which explains why business success is so elusive and complex. Suppose you are baking an apple pie. You have the perfect recipe. You've bought the same kind of apples Grandma used and they are precisely ripe. The dough is flawless, the sugar correctly measured, the pie tin perfectly proportioned and appropriately greased. The oven is preheated and the temperature accurate. The timer is set. But suppose that during the preparation a teaspoon of paprika was inadvertently added to the mix. Despite everything else being perfect, this one small slip caused the entire pie to be a disaster. The same is true for business. One tiny mistake can derail the entire process.

Finding the dash of paprika that is ruining your pie requires careful thinking and close observation.

CHAPTER 4

THINKING TIME: THE PROCESS

Designing a Thinking Time process that works for you will be no different than figuring out any other ritual you want to create. The time of day, the best location, and the optimum duration are all discovered through practice and experimentation until you have created a Thinking Time process that best supports your outcomes. The key here is to obsess about obtaining the outcomes and not about finding the perfect process!

My Thinking Time is based on many years of trial and error to find the exact combination that works for me. My strong recommendation is that you start with my process and adjust it to meet your needs.

My Thinking Time is highly ritualized. I have a thinking chair. The only time I sit in it is during my Thinking Time sessions. I have a thinking pen and thinking journal: I use them only when I am in Thinking Time mode.

And I follow this step-by-step process to structure each Thinking Time session:

1. A great Thinking Time session requires a great question as the launching pad. Prior to my Thinking Time session, I will create and write down a question(s) I want to think about. (In the

remainder of this book, you will find examples of various Thinking Time questions I have developed and used over the years.)

Often I create three to five questions that focus on a common thread or concern. Sometimes, during the actual Thinking Time session, I might change only one or two words in a question to see if I can get a different insight into the issue I am thinking about. For example, the original question might be: "Who is my target market?" I might change this to: "Who was my target market?" I could tweak this question to: "Who is my competition's target market?" That question could easily change to: "If I was starting again today, what market would I target?" I could add this question: "If I wanted to double my sales, what market would I target?" This might morph into: "Why aren't my sales double what they are right now in the market I am currently targeting?"

Each of these questions will spark different possible ideas, insights, and answers, which is why I am doing the thinking in the first place. I am not concerned about addressing each question on my original list. I might have three questions on my page, which morph into eight, but only make it through one. That's okay, because I am optimizing for possibilities, not completion.

2. I clear my calendar for sixty minutes, which will enable me to think for about three-quarters of an hour and then evaluate/ sort the solutions and ideas I identified in the last fifteen minutes or so.

3. I have three possible scenarios for my Thinking Time questions:
    *   Create a new question.
    *   Revisit a prior question that could use additional thought.
    *   Use an answer from a prior Thinking Time session as the basis for refining/fleshing out/changing the original question and searching for additional possible choices or variations on the theme.

4. For most of my questions, one Thinking Time session is insufficient, but focusing for more than about forty minutes is the limit of my capacity to concentrate. I will usually present myself with the same question (or with a possibility created in a previous session) over multiple Thinking Time sessions (two or three is not uncommon) before I get an elegant answer that is worthy of execution.

   I often have a Thinking Time session about the machine I need to create after I have of a viable solution. (In my Thinking Time, I am totally aware of the difference between an option and a choice: An option is an idea; a choice is executable. Each deserves Thinking Time.)

5. I close my door, turn off the phones, and eliminate all noise and visual distractions. I sit in my chair (which does not face my computer or a window), question, pen, and Big Chief tablet in hand. (I am old-school, so I always think on paper and never the computer, where too many distractions and temptations pop up.)

6. I set a timer on my computer that alerts me when my Thinking Time has expired and keeps me from fidgeting and looking at my watch.

7. Right before I start, I sip my water, scratch what itches, go to the bathroom, clear my throat, and then sit perfectly still. I have found over the years that my body has the power to derail my thinking and break my concentration. To optimize the thinking process, I must lose touch with my body so that my train of concentration is totally uninterrupted. During my Thinking Time, I am totally motionless except for my right hand, which is recording my thoughts.

8. I typically think with my left hand on my forehead partially shading my eyes, which limits my ability to get distracted by looking around my office and breaking my concentration.

9. In my Thinking journal I always have an empty *dot* ("."). It looks like this:

   Question: How would I run my business if 100% of my future customers were by referral only?
   - ABC
   - XYZ
   -

   The instant I write down an answer, I always create a new *dot*. My mind sees an empty "." and assumes there must be at least one more idea.

10. This is a creative process not intended to be filtered or judged. If I hit a blank or gap in which nothing is flowing (or my mind starts wandering), I will silently re-ask myself the question I am working on during the particular session. I might also silently ask myself, "What else could it be?" or "What could I do that would make this problem worse?" or "How would my competition solve this problem?" or "If I got fired and a new CEO took over, what decision would she make?"

11. Ideally, I let one idea spark another tangential idea and follow that train of thought as far as it wants to take me. I remind myself that I am looking for ideas and possibilities, not perfection and absolutes. I attempt to avoid judging my ideas (which I have found is almost impossible for me, but nevertheless is my goal). The more judgment I have about an idea during the actual Thinking Time process, the less creative and more prejudiced I tend to be.

12. Remarkably, I have found my better ideas tend to emerge during a pattern known as the "third third." The first third of my ideas on any given day are typically the obvious ones. The second third are variations on the first third. But the last third tends to be the most robust and frequently are where the juice is found.

13. When my Thinking Time has been successful, I'm always startled when the alarm goes off. I can't believe how quickly the time

has passed. At the conclusion of my forty to forty-five minutes of Thinking Time, I will always take at least fifteen to twenty minutes to read what I have written and capture the best ideas I have uncovered (usually no more than three).

14. Capturing my Thinking Time ideas while they are fresh is critical to this process. The key is to connect the dots, not just collect more dots. I have a separate file in which I keep my best ideas, insights, and distinctions. These ideas can become the basis for a future Thinking Time session or might need to marinate for a few days.

    If any of these ideas are worthy of future consideration or possible action, then I schedule additional Thinking Time on my calendar. If I don't take the step of scheduling it on the calendar, it stays on my "To Do" list and never gets implemented or addressed. (A handy tool I use for To Do lists is to identify the lingering items that keep getting transferred from list to list throughout the year and do a Thinking Time session on specific To Do items to figure out what needs to happen either to get traction or remove them from my list.)

15. It is rare for me to have fewer than two or more than three Thinking Time Sessions in a week. (Having said this, I could probably benefit from more.)

Fundamentally, Thinking Time is a structured process that enables me to minimize the risks, identify the opportunities, and maximize the results. That is a pretty high return for a very low-cost investment.

The following chapters in this book are from my Thinking Time library. Each chapter starts with some commentary, principles, or ideas and concludes with a series of Thinking Time questions for you to consider as fodder for your own next Thinking Time session.

It would be a mistake to simply read this book and put it on the shelf. The real value comes from doing the Thinking Time about the topics and questions presented.

CHAPTER 5

MMM . . . KOOL-AID

What we refer to as conventional wisdom rarely passes the sniff test of common sense. The recipes and "secrets" being peddled as THE formula for financial, business, and investing success are the leading cause of financial failure, frustration, and disappointment.

If you drank the Kool-Aid of one of these "how to get your mind right and passively become a millionaire in thirty days with no money down by working four hours per week from your kitchen table in your bathrobe" best sellers, chances are you are in worse financial shape now than when you started. At least before you bought the book you had the cost of the book in your wallet.

The problem is, the vast majority of these financial self-help gurus who promise millionaire, even billionaire, status owe their financial success to selling the Kool-Aid, not from drinking it themselves.

And, sadly, most of their disciples have a tendency to gravitate to the path of least resistance or the door marked "WOW!" Yet, when you think about someone you admire, someone who has achieved the success or greatness you aspire to, you will inevitably find years of practice, hard work, patience, persistence, correction, more practice, and more corrections. You will find a willingness to make mistakes and an uncommon ability to learn and course-correct as a result of those mistakes. (Learning doesn't happen until something changes.)

You will also find a teacher, coach, or mentor who illuminates the way so you do not have to make all the stupid and obvious mistakes yourself. What you will NOT find are overnight legends or effortless greatness, regardless of the field of endeavor. Gold medals are never won by the competitor who did the least or read a book on how to run a marathon and not get tired, much less worked only four hours a week.

When we really take a hard look at the people we want to emulate, we will inevitably find that they all started at the back of the line. They practiced for countless hours, stayed in line, followed the advice of a great coach or mentor, overcame numerous obstacles, had some lucky breaks, committed to being a learner, practiced countless more hours, and eventually got to the front of the line. Here is an important point: Their success was not obvious at the beginning of the journey—to themselves or anyone else who happened to be watching.

Check this out:

- Warren Buffett invested full-time in the stock market for nine years before he made his first million. I don't know anyone who would sign up for a course or read a book entitled *How to Make $1,000,000 in Only 9 Years*.

- In 1979, Bill Gates agreed to sell Microsoft to H. Ross Perot for *$20 million*. Perot backed out of the deal. Neither of them could see the upside. A $500 billion mistake for Mr. Perot.

- In 1998, Sergei Brin and Larry Page offered to sell their unknown start-up technology company to Yahoo! for $1 million so they could return to their studies at Stanford. Yahoo! passed. Four years later, Yahoo! realized its mistake and tried to buy Google for $3 billion, but the Google boys would only sell for $5 billion. Incredibly, Yahoo! passed again. Today Google is worth $600 billion. Given Yahoo!'s sorry current state of affairs, this is an especially poignant dumb tax.

- The first technology job Steve Jobs had was with Atari, the video game company founded by Nolan Bushnell. When Steve quit Atari to found Apple, he asked Nolan to invest $50,000 in his start-up in exchange for 33% ownership. Bushnell declined and missed out on a $275 billion profit. He was unable to see how this would ever work out to be a good deal.

Here is the message: Business is complex and the future is unknown. Tactical solutions, simplistic formulas, and generalized answers tend to cripple rather than enhance success. No one has all the answers and nobody can predict the future, including me. Whatever you do, *don't drink* my *Kool-Aid, either.*

On the other hand, don't ignore what I'm saying. Do some independent thinking for a change. Just because someone has written a book doesn't mean he knows what he's talking about. The same holds true for me.

Here it is on a bumper sticker: Be careful who you take advice from. Are they really an expert, or just someone with an opinion and a publisher? Be suspicious of one-size-fits-all solutions (I caution about this in the chapter "The Bathrobe Theory of Business . . . When a Good Idea Isn't.") Your situation is likely to be unique and require some serious brainpower to sort out the core problems and possible solutions. Be distrustful of advisors who predict the future. (As a Wall Street sage has quipped, "The reason God made economists is to make astrologers look good.")

Clearly, Bill Gates and the Google boys are grateful for the lack of clairvoyance of their suitors. (Perot and Yahoo! are still trying to forget their incredible misread of the tea leaves—and these are some smart people!) Be wary of experts who claim to have an abundance of answers (usually accompanied by a high degree of certainty) without an adequate understanding of your situation. Hubris, arrogance, and self-confidence on steroids are typically the breakfast of failure, not success. Great advisors (like great doctors) tend to do some serious diagnostics prior to reaching for the prescription pad. A world-class advisor will always tend to have better questions and far fewer answers than the run-of-the-mill quack. They know that knowing that they don't know everything is critical for controlling risks.

Here it is on a bumper sticker: Consultants have a recipe. Masters have a cookbook!

Thinking Time

- Where are we compromising by looking for the door marked "WOW!"?
- What shortcuts are we attempting to take that are not really shortcuts but rather mirages of greed, laziness, or impatience?
- What skills do I need to master to attain the success I want?
- Realistically, how much additional time and practice are required for me to attain my outcomes?
- Who can I hire as a coach or mentor to help guide me and hold me accountable?
- Where do I need to practice to improve my game and thus deserve the success I want?
- Where do we need to pick up the level of intensity in how we are playing this game?

NOW . . . Go Think! You will thank me later.
KJC

CHAPTER 6

THE 4 HATS OF BUSINESS

The vast majority of new businesses are started by people who are passionately in love with their "new" idea (the Artist/Creator) or who have a special skill . . . doctor, plumber, or shepherd (the Operator/Technician).

While passion and technical competence are extremely important, they are of primary value in the "getting traction" and "creating a niche" stages of growth. After a certain amount of time, size, and momentum, more passion and enhanced professional skills are not the primary drivers of growth and sustainable business success.

Artistic success requires refinement of creative and artistic talent. Operational competence requires honing professional and technical skills. *Business* success requires mastery of *business* skills and tools.

As a business grows (gets traction and scales), the additional skills required to evaluate and seize new opportunities, create enterprise value, and sustain momentum are all *business*-related: for example, managing cash flow, hiring the talent, reading financial statements, creating a culture, refining the target market, designing the messaging, leveraging other people, delegating tasks, allocating resources, prioritizing, strategizing, creating dashboards, and measuring outcomes.

When you stop to think about it, business success is really no different from any other kind of success. Mastery of the critical skills, strategies, and tools is mandatory. (See "The Big 8" for a description of the process that's key to moving from being an Operator to an Owner of a business.) If you want a gold medal in pole vaulting, mastering a badminton jump smash will be of little benefit. The critical distinction is an understanding of which gold medal you are trying to win.

If your dream is to become rich in *business*, then mastering *business* skills is compulsory. Notice I did not say, "Improving your product or becoming a better plumber is compulsory." There's a big difference between winning the gold medal as the best plumber in the world (artistic and operational achievement) and winning the gold medal of making $1,000,000/year of bottom line profit as the Owner of a plumbing business (business success).

Few things are more common than unrewarded artistic and technical expertise.

But that prestigious award will have virtually nothing to do with the size of your bank account or the enterprise value of your business. Look no further than boxer Mike Tyson, rapper 50 Cent, MLB pitcher Curt Schilling, or movie director Francis Ford Coppola. All were artistic and technical legends and all made a fortune with their unique skill and artistry. But, all went broke financially. The entrepreneurial curse is the naive belief that spectacular artistic success in one arena is transferable to another field. Or, as Bill Gates has quipped, "The problem with success is that it lulls smart people into believing they know what they're doing." I would say it a different way: The problem with karaoke is that just because you give someone the words doesn't mean they know how to sing.

In the world of business success, four primary roles *must be performed:* Artist (Creator); Operator (Technician); Owner (Business); and Board (Investor). At the beginning, when the business is smaller and lacks resources, the founder must fill *all* these roles, which is why small business owners are always tired and stressed. Over time, as the business gets mass and traction, additional personnel can be added to the team to leverage the performance of any or all these roles. The primary crisis of most start-ups and small businesses is usually cash, traction, or operational structure, any one of which causes the Owner (Business) and Board (Investor) roles to be ignored. A word of caution: Believing passion and operational excellence will trump business skills and risk assessment is a guaranteed prescription for a breathtaking dumb tax. (For more cautionary advice about the importance of evaluating risks, see the chapter "Not All Risks Are Created Equal.")

Think of each role as a different hat that must be worn, depending on what the business needs. When you add each hat to your wardrobe, it allows you to think about your business in different ways at different times. Sometimes you will need to create. At other times you must think in terms of risks or sales or dashboards. Wearing an Owner hat while in a creation mode or wearing an Artist hat while trying to assess the risks results in misguided and expensive mistakes. Having a hat for each role equips you to think about your business as a whole rather than just a set of discrete activities that must be performed.

Don't confuse these hats with your identity, though. They do not define who you are or what you are capable of doing, which means you are not stuck. No one "is" an Artist, but lots of people have significant artistic strengths. Having artistic talent is not mutually exclusive with learning how to read a balance sheet or delegating to your team any more than enjoying restoring vintage automobiles is mutually exclusive with your level of fitness.

These hats are interchangeable at will. But each hat requires a different mindset and skill set, both of which can be learned. (Here's another word of caution: The victim mentality of the what-you-see-is-what-you-get worldview is the perfect excuse to let you off the hook for taking responsibility for your business's outcomes and results. Don't let it. If you want *business* success, then learn the necessary *business* skills and tools.) There is no such thing as a rich victim.

On the following page is a diagram that outlines the primary focus, plan, strategy, outcome, and motto of each of the four hats.

	Artist (Creator)	Operator (Technician)	Owner (Business)	Board (Investor)
Focus	Passion	Value: Time + Effort	Value: Leverage + Measure	Value: Thinking + W.D.I.S.?
Plan	Create It (Fun)	Control It (Sweat)	Structure It (Machine)	Keep It (Sustainability)
Strategy	Start It (I ♥ My Idea)	Do It (React)	Lead It (Coach)	Sustain It (Defense)
Outcome	Fulfillment (Hobby)	Business Runs You	You Run the Business	Asset Allocation + Risks
Motto	"If it's not fun, I'm not doing it"	"If it's going to get done, then I'll have to do it."	"Measure Results . . . Change Activities"	"Not so fast, Cowboy!" (The Power of 3)

NOTES:

W.D.I.S.? = What Don't I See? What no one can see is their assumptions. (Reread Core Discipline #3—Check Assumptions in the chapter "The 5 Core Disciplines of Thinking" for more insights about W.D.I.S.?)

The Power of 3 = These three questions should be asked prior to making any major business decisions and investment activities:

1. What is the upside?
2. What is the downside?
3. Can I live with the downside?

(See the description of Core Discipline #4—Consider the 2nd-Order Consequences in "The 5 Core Disciplines of Thinking" for more on this topic.)

ARTIST (CREATOR)

An Artist is highly creative. Artists *love* their ideas and their art.

They live to create art and find producing it highly energizing. Most artists would love to commercialize their work product and have millions of customers applauding its creativity and beauty, but they make the faulty assumption that the key to more applause and higher sales is tweaking the product. In other words, if they could only improve their art, they could make more money.

If McDonald's was run by an Artist, the management team would spend the majority of their time trying to create a healthier and better tasting cheeseburger. (Clearly, the McDonald's Artist hat was abandoned years ago.) On the other hand, Steve Jobs was a full-blown Artist during his first tenure with Apple . . . and it almost destroyed the company. (It got so bad they had to get an investment from his nemesis, Bill Gates.) After his reinstatement as CEO twelve years later, Steve tempered his artistic flair with some business and risk assessment acumen (Board hat), which allowed him to successfully create one of the greatest businesses of this century.

An interesting aside is this: artists and operators tend to be control freaks. **Here it is on a bumper sticker:** Unfortunately, growth and control work inversely. The more growth you desire, the less control you can have (and vice versa).

OPERATOR (TECHNICIAN)

An Operator is a great Technician who adds value through time and effort. Operators focus on getting it done. The erroneous belief is that the harder they work, the more they will make.

For all their initial optimism and grand plans for global domination, the bulk of all operators find themselves in a defensive mode, reacting to the problem du jour. New ideas and opportunities are difficult to take advantage of because there simply is no time. Most operators spend so much time racing around putting out fires they never have the chance to figure out who is starting them. The Operator is not running the business; the business is running her. More often than not, when Operator-driven businesses fail, it is because the Operator has died of exhaustion. (For words of caution on this matter, refer to the chapter "Opportunity Without Structure Is . . .")

OWNER (BUSINESS)

An Owner is engaged and involved in the planning, execution, measurement, and corrections necessary to proactively lead and manage the business and employees. Owners add value primarily through leverage (team) and measurement (dashboards and financial analysis). Growth and control are balanced because the rules of delegation (vs. abdication) are being followed.

An Owner focuses on creating a structure or machine that relies on various moving parts all synchronistically doing their job to achieve a common outcome. Like a coxswain for a sculling boat or the conductor of an orchestra, owners establish the direction, unify employees, set the tempo, listen critically for the beat and performance of each team member, and correct/coach mistakes as necessary. ("The Big 8" provides more details about each of these functions within a business.)

A great Owner runs the business end of the business by measuring results and then either fertilizes the activities that produced the good results or changes the activities that caused the bad ones. Owners know and use all the levers in the business cockpit—particularly the financial statements, dashboards, and metrics of the business—to help them make great decisions. (For additional insights on the value of the "leverage and measurement" focus of the Owner's hat, see my book *The Ultimate Blueprint.*)

Board (Investor)

A valuable Board of Directors uses the same skill sets and brain cells as a great Investor does. The key attributes of both are the abilities to question, probe, think sequentially, substitute rational thought for emotion, anticipate crisis, predict 2nd-order consequences, and identify risks. Unlike the other three hats, which are focused on the "doing" part of business, the Board (Investor) hat is a way of thinking. This is the hat that all owners must have and use because it minimizes the likelihood of an interception or a fumble at critical junctures in the game.

The problem is that diagnosing your own disease, correcting your own golf swing, or defending yourself in a courtroom are impossible to do well; there's too much emotion, not enough perspective. Doctors seek advice and second opinions from other medical specialists. Every serious golf professional will hire a coach to watch her swing. Attorneys who find themselves on the wrong end of the legal system will hire a defense lawyer to represent them in a trial. A Board of Directors serves as a coach/trusted advisor to the CEO. How members of the Board think and what they think about is something every CEO/Owner should emulate, whether or not they have a formal Board. The vast majority of large, successful companies added a Board of Directors early in their trajectory. Filling this vital role is an integral part of the journey that must be traveled to avoid misguided, overly enthusiastic, irrational lurches that create dumb tax and slow value creation and growth.

I will say this a different way: The majority of dumb taxes incurred are a direct result of having only one voice in the conversation when the original decision was made. Adding experienced, wise, thoughtful, trustworthy voices to the conversation exposes risks, curtails faulty assumptions, and minimizes stupid.

The single best business decision you will ever make is to intentionally work with a peer group on a regular basis to question assumptions, ask hard questions (the kind you hope nobody will ask), alert you to icebergs, raise the bar, and push and hold you accountable. (See appendix 2, Board of Directors, for our invitation to join one of our Board of Directors.)

While an Artist is "creating" it, an Operator is "doing" it; an Owner is "leading, structuring, and leveraging" it; and the Board is protecting the business and keeping it alive.

A Board knows that business is an intellectual sport and that championship teams always have a world-class defense. Therefore, a thoughtful, measured approach to decision making, risks, priorities, allocation of assets, assumptions, and 2nd-order consequences (What Don't I See?) is critical to avoiding the dumb tax and creating sustainable wealth.

Thinking Time

- If my business could talk, what would it say?
- Which hat has been my comfort zone and which hats are not getting worn often enough? For that matter, which hats do I not even own, and how can I acquire them?
- What, specifically, have I been ignoring about my business, and what specifically needs to be corrected?
- What skills or tools do I need to learn (or who do I need to hire) to help me overcome the obvious obstacles that are restricting my growth, sales, and profitability?
- What areas of my business could be delegated (or outsourced) to someone else (who is competent and has execution intelligence) to free me up to do the things that would add the most value?
- Artist Hat: What needs to be created?
- Operator Hat: What needs to be done . . . today?
- Owner Hat: What needs to be structured? Measured? Planned? Delegated?
- Board Hat: What could go wrong? How can I mitigate the probability of that risk occurring and, if it does occur, reduce the cost?

NOW . . . Go Think! You will thank me later.
KJC

CHAPTER 7

CULTURE IS KING (YOU GET WHAT YOU TOLERATE)

Have you ever hired someone and she didn't work out?

Remember how eager and optimistic this new employee was on her first day of work? She probably had laid out her clothes the night before, planned the best route to work, and was in bed no later than 10:00 p.m. in anticipation of the big day.

She set two alarm clocks "just in case" and both were set thirty minutes earlier than required. After a healthy breakfast, she left the house sooner than necessary because there might be traffic and arrived at work twenty minutes before the official starting time. Excited and not a little nervous, she was ready to go to work and make a difference.

Fast-forward ninety days. Sunday night dinner, a bottle or two of wine with her friends until 12:30 a.m. The next morning *one* alarm clock goes off and she gets a couple of extra groggy "snoozes" before stumbling into the bathroom for a quick shower. Make-up is tossed into her purse to be applied while driving. Breakfast is a roadie coffee to get the blood flowing, and she arrives at work ten minutes late. The first twenty minutes are spent gossiping with coworkers about their weekend, and finally, forty-five minutes after starting time, she tries to look busy by answering a few emails and checking her Facebook account.

What happened to cause this gradual deterioration during those ninety days? One word: Culture.

The culture of the company gradually taught her what was acceptable and normal. She learned the rules of the game and the minimum level of effort required to get by. She adapted to her new workplace environment by figuring out how things were done around here and she went with the flow.

The vast majority of business management teams—whether a publicly held Silicon Valley behemoth or a mom-and-pop Sioux Falls corner drugstore—have drunk the Kool-Aid that stocking the kitchen with free protein-enriched smoothies and heart-healthy pork rinds are drivers of culture. Having a corporate concierge service pick up your dry cleaning and arrange for a back massage do not promote culture.

Recently I heard an extremely well-known entrepreneur tell an audience that she is encouraging a great culture at her company by building two nap rooms for her employees. Seriously, nap rooms? She made the stupid mistake of thinking perks drive culture . . . and that is dead wrong. Perks are wonderful for employees, but they come closer to driving entitlement than culture. (Instead of nap rooms, it would have been far cheaper to stock the kitchen with Red Bull, but then again, why stock a five-hour energy drink if your employees are only going to work four?)

The problem is not limited to Silicon Valley. Look at any business magazine when they rank "The Best Companies to Work For." The litmus test is always based on perks, goodies, and benefits, not on culture, challenge, personal growth, or getting stuff done. The assumption is that more coddling equals happier employees. Dumb! That's analogous to saying more money can fix a broken marriage. More money might make it bearable, but it won't fix it.

Culture is not values or mission statements; those are ideals, not disciplines. Culture is how we treat each other, how we talk to each other, whether or not we trust each other, and how we handle conflict. Culture is about accountability, measuring, a bias for urgency, a focus on solutions, calling it tight—saying what needs to be said—being kind and generous, acknowledging one another, and expressing appreciation.

In case you doubt what I am saying, just take a look at U.S. Navy SEALs. They have one of the greatest cultures of all time and it is not because they get to bring their dog to work or have a nap room. They get stuff done, hold each other accountable, and work in unison for a common objective . . . and they are proud of their results!

All relationships—be it marriage, parent-child, boss-employee—operate within a culture. Regardless of the relationship, certain ways of acting and "showing up" are permitted and acceptable and others are strictly out of bounds and inappropriate.

The problem is that the culture we currently have in our workplace relationships is rarely a culture we consciously created. Rather, the culture in our businesses is a culture we have tolerated because of a lack of courage to address the problems of back-biting, smack, cliques, excuses, blaming, silence, gossip, procrastination, missed deadlines, being late (and unprepared) for meetings, mediocrity, and doing just enough to get by. (See "The Apology" for guidance on how to initiate a cultural change.)

Here it is on a bumper sticker: The key to a great culture is creating and fostering a never-ending conversation about the "rules of the game." The rules define the boundaries or guardrails so that everyone knows exactly how to act, how to communicate, and how to treat each other. Culture, not a value statement, is the key to high performance and becoming the employer of choice. (Enron's Value Statement was Respect, Integrity, Communication, Excellence. A plaque on the wall is not a substitute for culture, and neither are nap rooms.)

Culture is so important to me in the businesses we own that we include a culture statement in our job postings. We also spend a lot of time discussing our culture principles (rules of the game) in the first interview. No need for me to find out how talented you are if you are not a good fit with our culture. I always tell prospective employees that their talents and willingness to hit my outcomes is what will get them this job, but their ability to perform inside our culture is what will allow them to keep their job.

Rules-of-the-game conversations are a standard part of our employee coaching sessions, "town hall" employee meetings, and performance reviews.

Here is a copy of the message we require our headhunters to include in the job description for the search assignments for our businesses. We also use this exact language in our "Craig's List" ads.

If you can commit to and live with the following principles, then you are the type of person who will be successful and help our company thrive. If you feel this level of engagement is not right for you or that you're not willing or able to participate with us at this level, we are not a good fit for you.

Our expectation is that you will take the steps necessary to do what you say you are going to do and be accountable for your actions. In other words, live "Above the Line."

We understand that not every person is ready for this level of performance, and we appreciate the honesty of those who decide this is not the right place for them. On the other hand, you would make an ideal candidate to join our company if you are willing to commit to the following Above the Line principles:

- *Accountability: See It, Own It, Solve It, Do It*
- *Become part of the solution*
- *Respect for others and their feelings*
- *Act now!*
- *Ask the question: "What else can I do?"*
- *Ask the questions: "What coaching do you have for me?" and "What can I do better?"*
- *Personal ownership and pride*
- *Reject average*
- *Show others that you care*

Coaching teaches people how to improve their performance. Training teaches people what to do. Culture teaches people how to treat each other. Most of the employees we terminate are fired for a lousy attitude and a cultural miss, not because they forgot the skills that got them hired in the first place.

Here it is on a bumper sticker: Anyone who says customers are #1 has lost their mind! Employees are #1. Employees are the source of all value creation. Culture (not jelly beans in the kitchen) is the source for engaged, turned-on employees. Show me a disinterested employee and I'll show you a lousy culture, a weak leader, and a poor customer experience.

Warning: When you're about to initiate a cultural shift, be aware of these three common culture saboteurs:

> **Iceberg #1:** Deciding to change the culture within your business is not an initiative for the weak of heart or uncommitted. It is not something you do once and forget about (which is why so many companies substitute perks for culture; you only need to build the nap room once). Creating and sustaining a world-class culture is an ongoing but immensely rewarding initiative. It lowers turnover, improves efficiency, and makes the business a good place to work. Besides, it is the right thing to do.

> **Iceberg #2:** There is always at least one person on a team who thinks he is immune to the culture transformation conversation. This individual thinks the rules do not apply to him because he's "special" or critically important to the organization and, therefore, immune to the rules.

> This special person is usually the stud salesman, the programmer who has the source code in his head, or the long-tenured employee who has been with you since the beginning. Your tendency will be to make an exception for this critically important person and his special circumstances. You will attempt to do a "work-around" and find ways to accommodate or justify his behavior—all in the name of "We can't afford to lose him."

> Trust me when I tell you that you will talk, coach, train, beg, reprimand, tolerate, and hang on to this person for way too long. Ultimately, however, you will have a decision to make: "Do I abandon my culture initiative or do I suck it up and replace this jerk?" You cannot make exceptions when it comes to culture. I

guarantee that you will say, "What took me so long?" once the toxic employee is given the opportunity to seek employment elsewhere.

Iceberg #3: An unenforced rule is not a rule; it's a suggestion. Coaching your employees is of no value without consequences. If you lack the courage to have the hard, straightforward conversations, save your time and avoid initiating a culture transformation. Every failure of leadership has at its root a lack of courage.

Here it is on a bumper sticker: The reason we hesitate to have the hard conversations is because we don't care enough. If you truly cared enough, you would say what needs to be said. After all, how else are they going to improve and maximize their potential? Let me remind you that nothing can change until the unsaid is spoken.

There are no shortcuts for implementing and sustaining the culture in any relationship. In the final analysis, truly caring about the people is what drives and sustains culture and culture drives value creation. Peter Drucker said it best: "Culture eats strategy for breakfast."

Thinking Time

- What is the culture we have now? (Make a list of how people act and treat each other . . . both good and bad.)
- What is the culture we want to create? (Make a list.)
- If this were the worst, most toxic place on the planet to work, what would the culture look like? (Make a list so you can start thinking about the opposites.)
- What would the culture look like if we were to become the "employer of choice"?
- What are the culture deficiencies in our business that are preventing us from being high-performance vs. high-maintenance?
- What are the beliefs employees must have that have led to the culture we now have?

- What are the new beliefs employees must have to construct our new vision of how we treat each other and work together?
- What are the specific rituals we can create which will help reinforce and memorialize our new culture?
- What are the difficult conversations I need to have to reset our culture and create a high-performance team?
- What are the simple rules of the game we must adopt to create a culture in which our people are truly engaged, committed to excellence, and do their best work?

NOW . . . Go Think! You will thank me later.
KJC

CHAPTER 8

GENERALIZATIONS KILL CLARITY

The primary reason most goals are never achieved and most budgets are never attained is because they are hollow, generalized statements of hope and not rigorous nonnegotiable standards, plans, and measurable drivers. (You'll see much more on these topics in "Cause and Effect.")

Here it is on a bumper sticker: Generalizations kill clarity. Clarity equals power. Power is the ability to act. Whenever there is weak, ineffective, or no action, it is usually a result of a lack of clarity and/or accountability. (A Board of Directors is great at filling this role.)

Most business owners and management teams are ineffective because they tend to use fluffy, glossy, generalized hand-waving as a substitute for a measurable, quantifiable plan.

"I see no reason why we shouldn't be at $2,000,000 of revenue by next quarter" is an effective way to deceive yourself into believing you have an actual, visible target on the wall you are aiming at.

Although they appear to be insightful at first glance, the following phrases are equally fluffy and meaningless.

I'll know it when I see it.	Preferably we will ...
I'm trusting that ...	Get laser-focused on ...
Get the support of ...	Develop the structure for ...
Make progress on ...	Enhance our marketing ...
My intention is to ...	We are moving forward on ...
We hope to achieve ...	Our situation is complicated.
The majority of ...	My goal is to get back to where we were.
Get this to the stage of ...	
A big portion of ...	Improve the performance of ...
The assumption is ...	Redouble our efforts.

Vague or wishful thinking is analogous to shooting a bullet at a wall, then painting a bull's-eye around the hole and awarding yourself a gold medal for your marksmanship. Expert snipers paint the target first and then fire the bullet. They know the contest is won or lost by their ability to hit the target, not their ability to airbrush a result after the fact.

A statement of a plan should sound something like this:

Here are the specific, measurable steps I'm taking (broken down by week) and the milestones, timelines, resources, and personal calendar time I am committing to reach $2,000,000 in revenue this next quarter. These are the names of each lead in our funnel. This is who and how many I will call on this quarter. Here is the conversion percentage I will achieve. This is the monetary value of each transaction. Here are the exact things I will do and the specific results I will generate to make certain we achieve our $2,000,000 target. I'll be reporting on these three specific measurable things (A, B, C) next week, and you should hold me accountable for achieving all three.

Can you see the difference between this statement of a plan and the earlier proclamation "I see no reason why we shouldn't be at $2,000,000 of revenue by next quarter"? We live in a world where accountability and measuring are feared and avoided. A lack of progress is excused because of heartfelt justifications such as: "You don't understand . . . I had this distraction . . . There was an unforeseen emergency . . . We tried really hard . . . Something else came up . . . They just weren't in a buying mood . . . This was harder than I thought it was going to be . . . My situation is complicated . . . The dog ate my . . ."

As one of my original mentors told me years ago when I tried to explain why I had missed a critical deadline: "Keith, good intentions do not achieve results. You have just given me some great *excuses*, but no good *reason* for why you missed having this ready for me." OUCH! Lesson learned! I will remind you that creating the plan does not cause the outcome to miraculously materialize. In fact, the actual plan will likely be missed . . . but having a specific measurable plan enables you to have the optics required to see the deviations in real time and course correct accordingly. (Though it sounds ironic, the chapter "It's Not About the Plan" emphasizes the value of planning and having one.)

A delicious meal is a direct result of following a specific recipe during the preparation, not envisioning the guests' applause after they've eaten it. When the food doesn't turn out as planned, you know the recipe was not followed.

Without a specific recipe, how can you anticipate what ingredients to buy and what cooking utensils you must have in your kitchen prior to starting to cook? (In business, these ingredients and utensils are called human resources, training, investment capital, and equipment.) Asian fusion at a five star restaurant is very different from chili cheese dogs at a ballpark, but both can be called dinner.

A plan is always executable (think cookbook or Google Maps). The key questions to ask in preparing to create your plan always start with How, What, or Who.

- How will we achieve this outcome?

- What specific activities are required to be performed?

- Who is going to perform them?

- What are our standards of performance?

- What are the critical drivers that must be consistently executed to achieve this outcome?

- How frequently must these critical activities be measured and reported to be successful?

- Who owns this outcome?

Here it is on a bumper sticker: Glossy and fluffy are always safe (and always produce mediocrity). Specifics and accountability require courage. A plan without specificity of deliverables and dates is a fantasy. Accountability should never be feared; it is the mother of great.

Thinking Time

- How do I need to rework our plans and budgets to make them granular and measurable?
- What is the specific recipe I need to create to make certain the outcome we have stated is achieved?
- What are the specific activities and milestones we must hit in order to stay on track with our stated deliverables?
- Who, specifically, is accountable and responsible for achieving each outcome?
- What are the dashboards I need to create to make sure we are measuring the critical drivers and making corrections based on our performance?

NOW . . . Go Think! You will thank me later.
KJC

CHAPTER 9

A CEO SHOULD *NEVER* DELEGATE . . .

While there have been an astonishing number of scholarly articles and books written about leadership, most of the academic focus is on the character traits, communication styles, or personality types of a successful CEO. As important as these attributes are, the reality is that a successful CEO has seven primary, non-delegable jobs. If these jobs are not successfully executed, the CEO will be ineffective, regardless of her charisma or Rorschach test.

1. **Clarity on Point A *and* Point B:** The CEO is solely responsible for understanding and articulating the reality of where the business is today (Point A) and the vision of where the business should be in the future (Point B). Candidly, the most difficult analysis required in #1 is an honest assessment of Point A. Business owners are fairly accomplished at describing the dream, but clarity about reality is rare. If your desire is to go to New York City, it is mandatory that you know if you are starting in Hong Kong or Hoboken. Different resources and timelines are required depending on where you start. ("It's Not About the Plan" provides my insights about this critical topic.)

2. **Identify the Gap and the Obstacle:** Without a clear grasp of Point A and Point B, there is zero likelihood you can describe the gap between your current reality and your desired outcome. The obstacle is buried within this gap. There is some obstruction (defined as the problem) that is blocking the attainment of the desired outcome. If there was no obstacle, you would already be there, and you're not, so there is. Understanding exactly what is obstructing your progress and defining this as a solvable problem (opportunity) dictates priorities and allocation of resources. (Reread the basics of Core Discipline #2—Separate the Problem from the Symptom in "The 5 Core Disciplines of Thinking.")

3. **Design the Plan and Machine:** With the obstacle clearly defined, a CEO can delegate and coordinate the design of the plan and the blueprint of the machine, which will allow the organization to overcome the obstacle and get from here (Point A) to there (Point B). Building a machine for the problem that isn't is a complete waste of time and money.

4. **Allocate Resources:** All machines consume resources. A CEO's job is to allocate the business's resources in a way that permits the business to stay afloat and simultaneously overcome the obstacle that is preventing attainment of the desired outcome. This is a massively tricky undertaking. It cannot be all one thing and none of another. Bills must be paid, employees nurtured, and customers served while simultaneously building the machine to overcome the obstacle in the way. In other words, the CEO must plan tomorrow's breakfast while continuing to cook tonight's dinner.

    Hint: A shift in priorities without a simultaneous shift in resource allocation is delusional. Anytime we announce new initiatives or change priorities, it requires a change in how we are allocating our resources (team, time, and money). It also requires that we do less of one thing to allow us to do more of something else. None of us has the ability to keep adding without curtailing or stopping something else.

5. **Top Grade for A Players:** Machines do not operate themselves. The caliber of your team is the single most important component of successfully and efficiently operating the machine, yet it is the one element where business owners tend to make exceptions and tolerate mediocrity. The players on your team are responsible for the vast majority of your leverage and ultimate success. Lousy players, poor leverage. Said another way, business success is highly dependent on who you hire and who you don't fire.

   All A players have six common denominators.

   a. They have a scoreboard that tells them if they are winning or losing and what needs to be done to change their performance. They will not play if they can't see the scoreboard.

   b. They have a high internal, emotional need to succeed. They do not need to be externally motivated or begged to do their job. They want to succeed because it is who they are . . . winners. People often ask me how I motivate my employees. My response is, "I hire them." Motivation is for amateurs. Pros never need motivating. (Inspiration is another story.) Instead of trying to design a pep talk to motivate your people, why not create a challenge for them? A players love being tested and challenged.

   c. They love to be measured and held accountable for their results. Like the straight-A classmate in your high school geometry class, an A player can hardly wait for report card day. C players dread report card day because they are reminded of how average or deficient they are. To an A player, a report card with a B or a C is devastating and a call for renewed commitment and remedial actions.

   d. They have the technical chops to do the job. This is not their first rodeo. They have been there, done that, and they are technically very good at what they do.

   e. They are humble enough to ask for coaching. The three most important questions an employee can ask are:
      * What else can I do?

- Where can I get better?
- What do I need to do or learn so that I continue to grow?

If you have someone on your team asking all three of these questions, you have an A player in the making. If you agree these three questions would fundamentally change the game for your team, why not enroll them in asking these questions?

f. They see opportunities. C players see only problems. Every situation is asking a very simple question: Do you want me to be a problem or an opportunity? Your choice. You know the job has outgrown the person when all you hear are problems. The cost of a bad employee is never the salary.

My rules for hiring and retaining A players are:

- Interview rigorously. (*Who* by Geoff Smart is a spectacular resource on this subject.)
- Compensate generously.
- Onboard effectively.
- Measure consistently.
- Coach continuously.

6. **Build the Organization Chart:** The people on your team operate within a structure called an organization chart. Structure is a requirement of turning chaos into opportunity and is the price for entrepreneurial success. The fundamental structure of a successful business is the organization chart because it defines who is responsible for every outcome and deliverable of the business.

In addition to having a conventional function/role/title org chart with boxes for who is in each role, consider creating an "Outcome Based Organization Chart" which has outcomes and deliverables in each box instead of titles and people's names. It will change the way you think about your business. (The chapter "Opportunity Without Structure Is . . ." is especially relevant on this point.)

7. **Create the Culture:** How people talk to each other and treat one another is the essence of culture—not how many jelly beans are in the kitchen or whether you can bring your dog to work. Jelly beans and dogs are perks and have nothing to do with culture. A great culture is based on showing other people that you care, accountability, measuring, and a desire for excellence. The CEO sets the example and the tone of the business culture. Show me a lousy culture and I will show you a lousy CEO. (Both "Culture Is King (You Get What You Tolerate)" and "The Apology" are worth taking a look at in this regard.)

Here it is on a bumper sticker: The key is the clarity on the obstacle and consistency of disciplined execution on the critical drivers. Consistency requires measurement. Discipline requires standards. Execution requires resources.

Thinking Time

- In light of the seven fundamental jobs of a CEO, where have I dropped the ball and what do I need to do differently to cause us to get better? (Nothing changes if nothing changes.)
- As I am thinking about the next 100 days and what I will do differently, what are the things I must do less of to make room for the things I need to do more of?
- If my team represents my leverage, what do I need to do or say to ensure *their* success?
- Starting and perfection are rarely simultaneous. What are the three things I could begin doing that would get me 80% of the way there?
- What is the discipline I need to adopt to create the outcomes I want?
- What is my specific measurable plan to improve our results?

- Where have I abdicated my responsibilities as a CEO and what do I need to do about it?
- Where have I optimized for easy instead of outcomes?

NOW . . . Go Think! You will thank me later.

KJC

CHAPTER 10

A CRISIS IS A TERRIBLE THING TO WASTE

In the late 1980s, as the real estate market in the Southwestern part of the United States collapsed, I was wiped out, as were many of my friends and business associates. We were experiencing the inevitable catastrophic aftermath of one of the greatest real estate booms in the history of mankind.

We had made scores of millions in the preceding six to seven years and subsequently had successfully lost every last penny we had—and then some. We had truly unmanageable debt loads. Twenty-four months previously, our property was worth two to three times the debt. In 1989 it was worth 20% of the debt, and the amount of debt had not gone up. The property value had been whacked by 80–90%. (Imagine more than 3,500 banks disappearing in a four-year time period, commercial real estate that could be bought for 20% of replacement cost, and rents for Class-A office buildings being less than the taxes/insurance and common area maintenance fees. This was our reality.)

We had no cash or cash flow, and we all had personal liability that far exceeded the market value of our assets. We were stone-cold broke, with no possibility of recovery. The hole was too deep.

Of even greater significance was the hit our egos had taken. Our identity was wrapped up in our financial success: When the success vaporized, so did our sense of who we were and what our place was. We were broke and broken.

We needed to heal, recover, and rebuild—but do it differently next time. We wanted to be certain that we NEVER had to experience this kind of disaster again. The thinking was not that we could somehow control the economy or interest rates. We couldn't. But what we could control was the thinking, disciplines, and strategies that allowed us to get caught in the tsunami in the first place.

We knew that if we didn't learn the lessons, we would be doomed to repeat them . . . an unacceptable possibility given the pain we were in.

We decided to pool our collective lessons learned (or been reminded of). We needed to make sure we accumulated twenty years of experience and not one year's worth of experience twenty times.

As you read the lessons collected almost three decades ago, you might be tempted to say this doesn't apply to you because you're not in the real estate business or because you're not doing big deals. I can assure you the lessons are applicable regardless of the industry or the size of your business.

Here it is on a bumper sticker: The best time to learn the lessons (and avoid the dreaded dumb tax) is prior to making the mistake in the first place.

Interestingly, most of us avoided repeating these mistakes in the ensuing twenty-eight years. Not because we were smart, but because the pain of the lessons was severe enough that we disciplined ourselves to avoid allowing our emotions to make what should have been intellectual decisions. We established a set of rules and disciplines and followed them maniacally.

Here it is on a bumper sticker: Making mistakes is inevitable; admitting them and learning the lesson is optional. I love what Dr. Buckminster Fuller said about this: "A mistake is not a sin unless it is not admitted."

Herewith are some of my favorite lessons collected during the week of February 20, 1989.

Log of Lessons Learned

Strategy

- A lack of rules, skepticism, and discipline caused every mistake we made.

- Emotions, when mixed with unbridled greed and easy access to capital, produce economic disasters.

- Financial engineering and incremental debt do not turn a bad deal into a good one.

- Raw land eats three meals per day.

- Catching a big wave is not the same as being a good swimmer.

- There is no way to correct without divorcing the story and marrying the truth. Facts do not cease to exist just because you ignore them.

- A good market tends to hide mistakes. Nothing takes the place of being actively engaged in the running of your business and being thoughtful (as well as skeptical) about the future.

- Last week's marketing report has absolutely nothing to do with where the market is headed, what the economy is doing, or what the demand will be next year.

- How you run your business during the good times is the only true predictor of how well your business will cope with the bad times.

- You must keep a conservative strategy during the good times because you generally don't know you're in bad times until it's too late.

- No team has ever won the game with an "offense only" strategy. Great teams, the ones who win championship rings, all have fantastic defenses. They think about prevention, protection, and risks.

- Not all progress is measured by ground gained; sometimes progress is measured by losses avoided.

- Speed kills. True wealth is built slowly. Speed and greed necessitate aggressive leverage and increase the odds of catastrophe. It is better to go slower and avoid the do-overs.

- Our desire for growth and size was based on ego and greed, not strategy and wealth.

- The successful people we admire are not the ones who made it. We admire the ones who kept it.

- Owners MUST be hands-on and involved in every aspect of the business.

- We acted like it was a sin to miss a revenue opportunity. That makes as much sense as needing to eat everything at a Sunday buffet.

- Do not be afraid to say "no." Saying "yes" does not always equal more.

- It's delusional to believe our ability, intellect, and work ethic can overcome a bad market.

- Litigation is expensive, time-consuming, and to be avoided.

- The best way to avoid losses and to stay financially healthy is to "sell too soon." The old real estate maxim "In the history of the world, the seller is always wrong" is outrageously stupid when you run out of cash!

- Don't fall into the trap of believing you can sell it for a higher price tomorrow. The future is unknown (and unknowable) and fraught with risk.

- In the future, I would rather miss an opportunity than lose capital.

- Never buy something because you think you might need it someday.

- Keep working all your alternatives until something closes. It hasn't closed until the money is in the bank.

- Success does not make you invincible or bulletproof. What success does best is make you complacent and egotistical, which by themselves are sufficient to create disaster.

- The euphoria of a hot market usually results in ignoring marketplace fundamentals. Prudently gathering and evaluating market-based economic information is the only prescription for avoiding the mistake of smoking your own exhaust.

- Never delay taking corrective action once the problem has been recognized. Hoping for better conditions in the future so the problem will solve itself is a fool's game. Procrastination magnifies problems.

- Failure to recognize reality is delusional. You might be smarter and better than your competition, but when the market shifts, you're still broke. Don't confuse intellect with economic reality.

- Never rely on only your consultant's recommendations. If you don't understand it, don't do it.

- We did not narrow our focus when we knew times were getting worse. This was due to two things: (1) The distraction of our prior track record, and (2) An unwillingness to assess the risks of being wrong.

- A small percentage of a large number is a large number.

- Any fool can make money in the good times.

- The question should never be, "Should I pursue this opportunity?" The right questions are:
  - If I pursue this opportunity, how much time, resources, effort, and investment are required?
  - Is this in my wheelhouse (core competence)?
  - What could go wrong?
  - What are the returns if I am right and the costs if I am wrong?
  - Can I live with being wrong?

- The greater the past success, the greater the likelihood of the Superman fantasy. A lack of cash or cash flow is Kryptonite and it kills all superheroes. Always be skeptical and keep some powder dry.

Deals

- Doing a deal to keep the staff busy is stupid. Do not do marginal deals.

- A bad economy doesn't create financial problems; it just reveals them.

- Almost everything takes longer than you think it will and costs more than originally budgeted. Plan for delays and bumps.

- Just because prices have gone up the last several years doesn't mean they can't go down 30% next year.

- The easiest sale is to an employee or a consultant.

- When the market is bad, there are NO buyers . . . at any price.

- Delaying the decision to sell today because last year's prices were higher or because the anticipated profits originally projected were greater is stupid. The market doesn't care about either.

- Do not follow the market down. Make deep cuts quickly.

- Don't let what your competition is doing influence your decisions. You can't erect a fence to keep the competition out. Besides, they do stupid things sometimes too.

- Secondary locations always decline the fastest (and most) and take the longest to return.

- New projects must be based on current demand and not future growth.

- You do not have to swing at every pitch that is thrown. Do fewer, better deals. Not only will you optimize the results of the superior deals, you will also have far less overhead.

- Too many deals consume time and draw attention away from the really good ones.

- It takes three good deals to make up for one bad deal.

- When a bad deal surfaces, 90% of management's time is siphoned off from the rest of the business to deal with the problems it generates. The result: The bad one is still bad and the good ones are now mediocre or troubled as a result of a lack of attention. Ninety percent of management's time should be spent on nurturing the good ones. Easy to say, hard to do.

- Holding off on adjusting the price or overhead based on the belief the market will rebound quickly is irrational.

Financing

- Debt gives the illusion of wealth. True wealth is assets, cash flow, and manageable (minimal) debt.

- Excessive debt and hope are the root of all financial crises. You can never ignore risks or suspend doubt.

- Doing a marginal deal just because the money is available is stupid. Bankers typically can't assess the market risks either.

- Take your personal guarantee seriously. You only bring two things to the table: cash and your guarantee, neither of which has an unlimited supply.

- Don't rely on future price increases to make a deal work.

- Never finance long-term assets with short-term debt.

- We covered a lot of mistakes with access to an abundance of money and easy credit.

- Too much money makes you stupid. Just because you can doesn't mean you should.

- Stretching to do a deal by horsing the numbers in a spreadsheet is usually a sign of ego and rarely a good idea.

Personnel

- Bench strength is critical. Find the best people and compensate them VERY well. It saves money in the long run.

- The tougher the times, the better the people you need. There is no way to survive a bad market with weak people.

- Adding/keeping mediocre people weakens the organization, which dilutes your results.

- Always be upgrading your talent and never be afraid to pay them what they need to make.

- Every hire we make should raise the average.

- One superstar 7-footer is far more valuable than ten 5-footers. Weak people beget weak results.

- Never wait to address personnel issues or substandard performance. Employees are either doing a great job or they aren't. If they aren't, take action. My job isn't to babysit or beg people to do their jobs.

- The cost of tolerating an incapable or misplaced employee is far greater than the discomfort of having a tough conversation and speedy termination.

- A culture rooted in past successes, growth at all costs, and aggressive bonus structures will produce employees who don't think, who aren't skeptical, and who ignore risks.

Overhead

- Stay lean even if you can afford to get fat. Keep overhead low!

- Watch your cash VERY closely. Ask yourself, "Do I really need this? Will this help me make more money?" Once the money is spent, it's gone forever.

- Get really sober (medieval) on what needs to happen to your cost structure to produce the profits you want vs. the revenue you hope to get.

- Each line item of your financials should be scrutinized on a continuous basis to make sure the money is being spent in a productive and prudent way.

- Conserve cash, especially during the good times. Spending money to look like a big deal is not the same as being a big deal.

- When you're out of cash, you're out of business. Cash is truly KING.

- When the market shifts, you can't cut overhead fast enough.

- It is easy to overpay or beef up when the world is viewed from only an upside perspective.

- Cut overhead early and hard. Pride and hubris kept us from cutting our overhead in a timely manner.

- Fancy offices, hot cars, lots of staff, and high overhead are signs of significance, not success.

- Knowing your numbers—what it costs to run each aspect of your business—and having timely information are critical to success.
- Focus on the costs of doing business and not just the revenue potential.
- Paying for overhead we don't need to support revenue we don't have is stupid.
- Contract out as much of the work as possible. Keep overhead low and variable.

Thinking Time

- As I look back at my most significant losses, stupidest decisions, and biggest mistakes, what are the fifty most important lessons I have learned?
- Where am I making some of these same mistakes again?
- Based on prior lessons learned, what do I need to change (immediately) to avoid the dreaded dumb tax?
- What are the rules and disciplines I will put in place to minimize the likelihood of repeating my mistakes?

NOW . . . Go Think! You will thank me later.
KJC

CHAPTER 11

ORDINARY THINGS, CONSISTENTLY DONE, PRODUCE EXTRAORDINARY RESULTS!

Think about one thing that you are really good at. Ask yourself this question: "How did I get good at this? Was it a result of some humongous thing I did last Tuesday?" Doubtful.

The fact of the matter is that anytime we start something new, we generally suck at it. We get good at stuff as a result of practice, mistakes, correction, more practice, more mistakes, and more correction. I will remind you that the intensity of your practice is a critical driver of the speed at which you attain proficiency or mastery. Dabblers do everything pass/fail . . . and usually fail.

Here it is on a bumper sticker: Ordinary things, consistently done, produce extraordinary results! Think about the discipline of consistently reviewing your prior month's financial statements by the 10th of every month. In a matter of a quarter or two, the insights and optics harvested will change the priorities and decision making in your business.

Think about one of your bad habits or business practices that is sabotaging you. Is this habit the result of some ginormous thing you did a couple of days ago? Doubtful again. It was an *ordinary thing, consistently done.* A track record of inconsistent and sloppy team meetings with wandering agendas and no accountability is a bad habit. Like all bad habits, it feeds on and reinforces itself unless it is consciously changed. The change requires courage and a certain degree of discomfort, but as with all decisions to address a bad habit, they are worth it in the long run.

Unfortunately, the root of most if not all my problems is the need for instant gratification. More often than not, if it doesn't look the way I thought it was supposed to look when I thought it would look that way, I get discouraged and quit . . . or start looking for another magic pill. Think of this as both an expectations and a timing issue. When we're dieting, we aren't disappointed when we haven't lost five pounds *in a single afternoon,* but if we expect to do so within one week and it hasn't happened, we cave. Faulty expectations coupled with unrealistic time frames kill dreams.

We self-sabotage when we look for the one massive thing that can be the game changer. We tend to want the results immediately. We want to get from where we are to where we want to be in fifteen minutes—no fuss, no muss, no sweat.

When you stop to think about it, the world is not designed to give us instantaneous feedback and results, either good or bad. You don't get lung cancer after just one puff. You don't gain thirty pounds after eating just one donut. You don't get into financial hock to the tune of tens of thousands of dollars of credit card debt in a day. So, it's irrational to believe that you will unwind these problems in the blink of an eye.

The results in your life so far—both the good results and the ones you would like to see changed (the ones you made your New Year's resolutions for the last couple of years)— happened as a result of continuous, steady, consistent daily actions. Changing these results requires different continuous, steady consistent daily actions.

Thinking Time

- Trying to figure out how to immediately solve a problem in one fell swoop is stupid. I might not have the final "Holy Grail" solution to all my problems, but what are five things I can do immediately to improve my situation?
- Where am I inconsistently executing the right thing?
- Where am I *not* practicing with the level of intensity I know I am capable of?
- Where are we practicing but not correcting or getting the coaching that would give us insights about what we can do better?
- Where am I consistently executing the wrong thing?
- Where have I allowed the need for instant gratification to become a substitute for picking up the business end of a shovel and consistently breaking a sweat?
- What are three outcomes we previously set but have abandoned because of unrealistic expectations or inconsistent execution? Should any of these outcomes be resuscitated and reprioritized with the accompanying realistic plans, resources, and time frames?
- What are three bad habits/business practices we have tolerated that are undermining our results?
- What are the decisions I must make and the hard conversations I must have to break these bad habits once and for all?
- How will I adjust my behavior to create the success/outcomes I envision?

NOW . . . Go Think! You will thank me later.
KJC

CHAPTER 12

O BABY!

My first date with Sandi was the world's greatest first date. We agreed to meet for dinner at a very nice restaurant in Austin, Texas. As the evening progressed, the range and depth of our conversation was surpassed only by my increasing attraction.

Three hours later I decided to take a rather large risk and venture into uncharted territory. "I am about to ask you a question I've never asked another woman in my whole life," I announced. Sandi cocked her head, braced herself, and said, "Okay. What?"

"What do you want?" I asked.

"What do you mean?" she replied.

"What do you want in a relationship? In a man?"

Without a moment's hesitation she said, "I want to be loved and adored."

I signaled to our waiter that I needed a pen and a piece of paper. I wrote at the top of the page: JANUARY 4, 2001—SANDI . . . LOVED AND ADORED.

"Now, tell me everything that needs to happen and exactly what it would look like for you to feel loved and adored." She talked (and I wrote) nonstop for an hour and a half. I had no idea one woman could want this much! This was clearly going to be high maintenance and I loved it!

One of the things Sandi wanted was a note every day . . . every day! When she said that, I literally could not force myself to write it down.

"Every day? You must be kidding me. That's a lot of pressure . . . *Every* day? What if I forget?"

Sandi smiled and replied mischievously, "I will remind you."

If you had asked me to try to conjure up the key to this woman's heart, it never would have entered my frontal lobe that it would be a note every day.

We have been partners and lovers ever since . . . and she gets an "O Baby!" (that's what we call the note) *every day*. She doesn't really care whether or not I'm "passionate" about writing daily notes. She just wants the note. It turns out that because Sandi loves getting it, I love writing it. (There is a lesson in here for you about pleasing your customers!)

Some of the notes are short, some are long. Sometimes they are romantic and sometimes they are downright nasty. (She didn't tell me what kind of note; she just said she wanted one every day.)

This story illustrates one of the most powerful principles to attract customers and gain significant traction in any business.

- **FOWTW:** Find Out What They Want. This is anticipating problems, identifying pain points, and discovering needs.

- **GAGI:** Go and Get It. This is design and build solutions for the problem/pain/need identified.

- **GITT:** Give It to Them. This is *how* you deliver a solution . . . the experience and execution.

Start with what *customers* want. Start with *their* needs, desires, and pain. Start with the gap between the solutions being offered by the competition and where *they* (the customers) are frustrated. We mistakenly start with what we want to sell without finding out if what we've "got" is what they "want." (I write about this at greater length in the chapter "Prioritizing Growth Strategies.")

When you start with what *you* want to sell, you are doomed to trying to jam what you've got down the customer's throat.

There are lots of good ideas about how to grow a business or expand market share; I've had a bunch of them myself. The question isn't whether I think I have a good idea. The questions are:

1. What do customers want?

2. Can I get them what they want?

3. How do I deliver it to them?

As Peter Drucker commented, "When marketing is done right, selling becomes unnecessary." And his definition of marketing? Finding out what customers want. (I miss Peter Drucker's wisdom.)

Thinking Time

- What do our customers want and how do I know that this is the right answer?
- What is the solution I need to design to meet their needs and address their pain?
- Do I have the ability (skill sets and resources) to successfully build this solution?
- How will I deliver it to them?
- What is the experience these customers want?
- What exactly is the gap between where customers are frustrated and what the competition is doing?
- Where can we find pockets of target customers who are frustrated with our competition?
- Where is the competition weak or deficient in delivering the outcomes, solutions, and value the market demands?
- What should we be doing to communicate to potential customers that we are the aspirin for their pain?
- What are the three primary problems (pains) my target market has?

- Where have I substituted my judgment for what I want to deliver for what the customers actually want to receive?
- How could I check in with our customers to find out what new pains they are experiencing or gains they want to achieve?

NOW . . . Go Think! You will thank me later.
KJC

P.S. I am fully aware that if Henry Ford had asked customers what they wanted, they would have said a faster horse. Most of us are not dealing in disruptive technologies. If you are, refine the questions I am suggesting so that you avoid the mistake of getting cool before you get clarity.

CHAPTER 13

HELP ME UNDERSTAND

Leading an organization is very different from managing one. Both require interaction and dialog with the team. Management's interactions usually take the form of being a sheriff. A leader's conversation sounds like a coach. ("The Big 8" chapter outlines a particularly useful process for managing the people and driving results in your organization.)

When we are disappointed with the performance of an employee, it's always a result of an unmet expectation. All upsets are simply unmet expectations.

The problem is that many of our expectations are also uncommunicated. We assume that the person has good judgment and thinks the way we do (can read our mind); therefore, explicit training, rules, and guardrails are deemed unnecessary. Bad assumption.

Great businesses have consistently high performance from their team. That's not an accident. These businesses have baked into their culture the rules of the game and expectations for what needs to happen to be successful at each job. They are crystal clear about what is expected and what is or isn't tolerated, and they coach to these outcomes. (A discussion about rules of the game can be found in the chapter "Culture Is King (You Get What You Tolerate).")

No one likes receiving a speeding ticket when there is no posted speed limit. If you want a high-performance culture, be very specific about what someone must do or how she must behave to be successful at your company.

When there is a miss on the performance, the conventional wisdom is to discipline the employee, especially if it is a second or third offense (sheriff).

Sometimes warnings and consequences are the appropriate and required form of communication. Unfortunately, a culture based solely on beating the noncompliant is a fear-based system and will never successfully engage the heart or engender the emotional commitment we all hope for from our employees.

Of course I want compliance, but I want the kind of compliance that is a result of ownership, accountability, and engagement, not fear of punishment and consequences.

I was reminded of this recently in a business we own.

One of our employees, Patty, is a cashier in this retail service business. In addition to taking customers' money and answering the phone, one of our cashiers' main areas of responsibility is making certain the lobby is clean and tidy for the hundreds of customers who walk through the lobby every day. (In case you weren't aware, the general public has a strong knack for creating a mess, especially if food and drinks are in the vicinity.) Patty knows what her job entails, has been trained repeatedly, and has been reminded more than once about the lobby being "under-serviced."

As I was walking through the lobby early one morning, I noticed things had reached the crisis state of pig. My first inclination was to discipline Patty with a verbal warning and an official write-up in her employee file with a note for severe consequences for failure to comply in the future.

My second thought was to remind myself that an official warning in her employee file justifies future dismissal but does not correct the underlying problem. I had fallen into the trap of thinking that we were on opposite teams and that Patty didn't want to be successful. I decided to fix the problem instead of fix the blame.

I corrected my thinking. Here is the conversation I had with her.

Patty, I think I owe you an apology. Apparently we have done a poor job of

- *Communicating what we want.*
- *Making sure you own the cleanliness of the lobby.*
- *Explaining why it is so important it be done a certain way.*
- *Providing you with the training you need for how to keep it clean.*
- *Tolerating what you have done in the past without giving you the appropriate coaching on how to do it better.*

I am very sorry.

What we expect is for the lobby to be kept clean and tidy, which means the floors are continuously monitored, swept, and mopped, the loose newspapers are thrown out, and the customers' seats in the waiting area are clean and organized. This is not happening on a consistent basis and is obviously not happening right now.

I am confused. Help me understand why I am seeing a mess in our lobby this morning. I know we have discussed this with you several times in the past, yet here it is again. Is the problem that

- *You don't understand what we want?*
- *You haven't been adequately trained?*
- *You just don't care what the lobby looks like despite this being a critical part of your job?*
- *We just got slammed with a bunch of customers and there hasn't been time to clean this up yet?*
- *You don't understand the importance of this job and doing it the way we expect it to be done?*
- *You don't own your job and are unaware of the consequences of not doing the job you were hired to do?*

Help me understand why this problem doesn't get fixed and stay fixed.

I waited for Patty's response, which turned out to be a weak, pathetic attempt to convince me that she didn't notice how messy it was, but now that I had pointed it out she realized it was obviously a problem.

Patty, you have a job here. To keep your job, you must do the work. The job and the work go hand in hand. It has now reached the point that it feels like we are begging you to do the work, which makes no sense because you never have to beg me for your paycheck. Neither one of us wants to beg, and neither of us should have to. You are a smart woman; you understand what we expect. But, for some reason it isn't getting done consistently.

Here is what I know: When my effort to help you get better exceeds your effort to get better, this stops working for both of us.

It seems to me the problem might have something to do with what you believe. For this to continue to be a topic of conversation, maybe you hear what we want but mistakenly believe what we are requesting is optional. Perhaps you believe we are just kidding when we tell you keeping the lobby picked up and clean is part of your job. You might believe we will not notice or, if we do notice, maybe you believe we will not say anything. You might believe you can avoid doing your job and we will pay you anyway, or even give you a raise for not doing your job. Maybe you believe that you can keep your job but not do the work. Help me understand what you believe about this.

I again waited patiently for her response. Ultimately she told me that none of these beliefs were true, to which I replied, "That's really good, Patty, because if any of those beliefs had been true and you were incapable of changing that belief, we would have to redefine our relationship. So, what is the belief you need to have about doing the work we have hired you to do?"

Fortunately for both of us, Patty figured it out. She now understands that I have a job that I hired her to do. This job entails doing certain work and producing certain outcomes. She understands that a job and the work are connected; if she doesn't do the work, she doesn't keep her job. She is the only person who can fire herself, and this unfortunate event can only happen if she decides not to do the work. She will know when she decides to fire herself because she will know she isn't doing her job, which requires her to produce certain outcomes.

Patty decided she needed to own her job and be responsible and accountable for her work. She understands that mistakes can happen, but when we miss, we own it and correct it immediately. She understands that the cleanliness of the lobby is no different from the cleanliness of the restrooms—both are a direct reflection on our company and how we do business.

With a little coaching, Patty figured out that since this problem wasn't getting and staying solved under the old way of doing it, she needed a different strategy. She came up with the idea that she needed a laminated checklist of all her job responsibilities to review periodically and a reminder system (we came up with an alarm on her iPhone that will beep every thirty minutes) to call her attention to the cleanliness of the lobby. If she is too busy with customers when the alarm sounds, we gave her a 911 process to call in reinforcements.

I strongly suspect I have saved a valuable employee. I think Patty wants to be successful and she now has the beliefs and a process that will support her in achieving our outcomes. I also suspect I have seen the last of the messy lobby area. I seriously doubt she wants to fire herself.

In dealing with employees, I have found one universal truth: They all want to be successful. The key is alignment on definitions of success. As a business Owner and leader, you must answer this question: What has to happen in order for this employee to be successful at his or her job?

The clearer we are on the coaching of *beliefs* and performance by shifting the burden of ownership and correction to the employee, the less the likelihood we will have to resort to begging, threats, and consequences.

Here it is on a bumper sticker: The only difference between a high-maintenance and a high-performance team is a culture of accountability, measuring, and ownership.

A footnote is in order for helping you coach and grow your team. When interacting with employees, the two most powerful phrases in a leader's vocabulary are:

1. Help me understand ...

2. What do you recommend?

Thinking Time

- Where have I done a poor job of posting the speed limit (explicitly stating expectations, deliverables, and outcomes)?
- Who are the people in my organization that seem to require repeat conversations about the same issue?
- What is the "belief coaching" they need to get clarity around the correct beliefs that will enable them to do and keep their job?
- What is the deliverable that is missing? What is the outcome I want that isn't being delivered?
- Where am I frustrated because an employee is not performing at the standard I expect (and set)?
- Is the problem that I haven't set a clear standard?
- Is the problem a lack of specificity about what I want it to look like? A lack of training? A lack of consistent coaching (calling it tight) when the problem arises? A lack of understanding about why this is important and why it needs to be done correctly every time?
- Where have I created (or tolerated) a culture of mediocrity, an absence of accountability, a fear of saying what needs to be said, and an inattention to results, measurements, and periodic correction?
- What is the belief my employees must have for this problem to persist and what belief needs to be substituted for my employee to excel?
- Who needs to get an apology from me?

- What is the coaching I need to deliver to make sure the problem gets fixed and stays that way?

NOW . . . Go Think! You will thank me later.
KJC

CHAPTER 14

OPPORTUNITY WITHOUT STRUCTURE IS . . .

Here it is on a bumper sticker: Opportunity without structure is chaos.

This one sentence summarizes the single biggest cause of frustration and exhaustion in the start-up and entrepreneurial business world.

You have a great product or professional competence that would be perfect for the market, so you decide to create a business around this idea. You always wanted to be your own boss, run your own business, call all the shots, set your own schedule, and be in charge of your future financial rewards.

But while you're in the process of perfecting the product, finding the customers, delivering the product, gaining traction in the marketplace, and producing revenue for your business, cracks start emerging in the back office.

The paperwork piles up. Customers become irritated with the lack of follow-through and unreturned calls. Scheduling and deadlines become spotty and delayed. Paying the bills gets relegated to a random Post-it note, which will soon be buried under one of the stacks of paper on your desk. The billing slips and the collection of A/R is deferred because there simply isn't time to do everything. Now cash starts to become an issue, so the decision is made to work harder and longer in the mistaken belief that you can brute force your way out of the hole. Dumb!

Over the last forty-five years of starting, buying, selling, financing, restructuring, and running businesses, I know firsthand the importance of leverage. In fact, leverage is the single greatest point of difference between owning a job and owning a business.

Leverage means doing more with less. At the beginning, business owners are compensated for their time and effort. But there is a limit to the amount of time we have available and the amount of effort we can exert. While mandatory at the beginning, time and effort as a long-term strategy results in a tired Owner and puny revenues.

Here it is on a bumper sticker: No leverage, no long-term growth. The inevitable result is chaos and a gravitational pull toward the urgent. Leverage is the bridge that transitions the Owner of a business from Operator mode to Owner mode. (For more Thinking Time possibilities, see the related chapters "YOU, Inc." and "On vs. In.")

When business owners think about leverage, they typically think about debt, which allows the business to do more with less equity. Of course, there are other forms of leverage, like adding support staff, networking, measuring, Thinking Time, and strategic alliances, to name only a few. (See my book *The Ultimate Blueprint* for lots more on how to measure results and use business optics to leverage the growth of your business.)

The leverage solution that is typically missed, though, is the leverage from structure.

Here it is on a bumper sticker: The price of entrepreneurial success is discipline and structure.

The problem is that most of us hate structure, which is one of the reasons we started our business in the first place. We want the "freedom" to do what we want, when we want. But freedom—just as entrepreneurial success—has a price: discipline and structure.

Being in business is hard, but without structure it is harder than it needs to be and substantially less rewarding than what is possible.

Structure means designing, planning, and constructing the skeleton of the business so there is a foundation and support configuration to enable the business to profitably take advantage of the opportunities available.

Structure might be systems, processes, and procedures. Or it might be rearranging the organizational chart, hiring the right people, and onboarding those people to be effective as soon as possible. Or it might be writing the training manuals on how things get done or creating the machine or the engine inside that machine.

Without structure, you feel as if every day is a race up a 200-foot-high sand dune—lots of slippage and little or no traction.

As difficult as this is for you to imagine, some people in this world love organizing and structuring things. It makes them crazy to see disorganization, a messy desk, and chaos. If structure is an issue you are grappling with (it is easy to detect because exhaustion, frustration, and inefficiency have become an epidemic), engaging or hiring these specialists can transform your business into a well-oiled machine.

Success is not an accident. Sustainable business success requires leverage, and one of the most critical forms of leverage available to a business Owner is the leverage of structure.

Thinking Time

- What is the structure we need to create the progress I want?
- What are the missing structural components required to produce consistent execution on our critical drivers?
- When I look at my business, where are the opportunities for me to tighten up the structure, processes, and efficiency of what gets done?
- Where do we have disorganization, inconsistent execution, slippage, and chaos?
- What are the obvious choke points in my business that continue to strangle the smooth operational flow of serving customers and supporting the back office?

- What specifically needs to happen to put some structure into place to address the turmoil?
- Is there an opportunity to hire someone (even part-time) to help fill some of our gaps or to support us in getting a process in place?
- What needs to happen to the workflow, back office, accounting, and support processes so my business functions smoothly and efficiently?
- Where is the structure of my calendar slipping that is preventing me from taking consistent action on my major initiatives?

NOW . . . Go Think! You will thank me later.
KJC

CHAPTER 15

MANN GULCH

On August 5, 1949, thirteen men died battling a relatively small blaze that turned deadly at Mann Gulch. Upon investigating the circumstances of why the majority of the smoke jumpers (firefighters who parachute into the back country to fight fires) died while only three lived, the U.S. Forest Service came to some startling conclusions.

The lessons they learned sixty-five years ago are universal and as relevant today as they were then, regardless of the "firefighting" we are doing.

Mann Gulch is a remote canyon surrounded by 1,200-foot cliffs in Montana's Helena National Forest. Many of these canyon walls are steep and treacherous to navigate in normal conditions, but the northern cliff is particularly difficult because of the 76° incline.

A small fire got started in the back woods at Mann Gulch and necessitated calling in the smoke jumpers to combat the blaze before it got out of control. As the sixteen men were battling the fire, the wind suddenly shifted and the fire expanded to 3,000 acres in a matter of minutes. The escalation and shift in direction trapped the smoke jumpers against the steep north face.

The smoke jumpers were in a race for their lives. To survive, they had to climb the nearly vertical northern wall of the cliff faster than the rapidly encroaching fire. One of the amazing things the Forest Service discovered was that the thirteen men who died had carried their cumbersome tools—poleaxes, saws, shovels, as well as very heavy backpacks—while attempting to outrun the fire up the face of the cliff. Even though their equipment was worse than useless in a footrace up the mountain, and it ultimately slowed and exhausted them, they had been trained to keep their equipment with them at all times. They literally died with their backpacks on.

For these firefighters, their tools represented who they were, why they were there, and what they were trained to do. Dropping their tools meant abandoning their existing knowledge, training, and experience. Their identity was at stake.

In hindsight, it seems obvious they made a catastrophic mistake in judgment, but because they hadn't been trained to think about outrunning a fire, they had no alternative models for behavior.

Here it is on a bumper sticker: When the environment radically changes and you are confronted with moments of uncertainty and danger, clinging to the old "right" way might seem like a good idea, but it can frequently be deadly. (For further insights, read "The Bathrobe Theory of Business: When a Good Idea Isn't.")

The three survivors of the blaze—one of whom was the foreman, Wagner "Wag" Dodge—were men who, when forced to rethink the real problem they were facing (in real time), came up with a solution. The problem was not how to put out or control the fire but rather how to escape from it and survive.

Dodge used a technique now known as an "escape fire," which was widely used by the plains Indians when trapped in a similar situation, but which had never been taught or used by the Forest Service.

Dodge struck a match and purposefully lit a ring of fire around himself. The fire he started burned the surrounding grass, providing him with a safe area in which to lie down. Since the area he burned had no remaining flammable grass, the main fire that was bearing down on him "jumped" over him and saved his life.

In the chaos and confusion of this tragic event, Dodge attempted to show his new idea to his fellow smoke jumpers, but they couldn't see how a burned patch of dirt was a solution for surviving the rapidly encroaching wall of flames, so they continued running up the steep slope.

Here it is on a bumper sticker: New circumstances always require new skills and tools, fresh training, innovative solutions, superior team members. The alternative (relying on past answers) is often a prescription for suffering and failure to survive.

Here it is on another bumper sticker: Sometimes the problem we started out to solve mutates. If we miss the shift, we will try to solve the new problem using solutions for the old problem. Chances are, those old solutions for the previous problem are useless.

Thinking Time

- What is the real problem I am facing and exactly how is this problem different from the one I thought I had? Or used to have?
- What are the poleaxes, shovels, and backpacks I've been lugging around that are no longer useful in helping me solve my immediate problem?
- What are the tired, worn-out strategies and plans that are no longer supporting us to solve the problem we face?
- What are the existing models of behavior we need to drop because they no longer work?
- What existing knowledge, training, or experience needs to be abandoned?
- What are the new, fresh ideas and solutions we need to create to get us past this problem and back on track to our desired outcomes?
- Survivors and successful people are always learning, innovating, and adjusting. If this statement is true, what do we need to learn and where do we need to adjust our performance to succeed?
- Who around me is screaming an alternative solution, but I am ignoring them because I don't see the problem or the need to shift strategies?

- Under the broad heading "What got me here won't get me there," who do I need on my team, who is excess baggage slowing me down, and what do we need to start doing differently?

NOW . . . Go Think! You will thank me later.
KJC

CHAPTER 16

DREAMS AND DEMAND

Our profits are suffering, so we set a goal to increase them. Employee morale is low, so we set a goal to have more "fun." Cash flow is weak, so the goal is to "improve" it. (For more about the fluff and nonsense in goal setting, see "Generalizations Kill Clarity.")

When it comes to goals, far too much emphasis is placed on visualizing Oz and not enough on designing and constructing the yellow brick road. Goals are not plans. Goals are ideas, and few things are dumber than executing on an idea with no plan or planning. It does no good to set a goal and then not create a specific plan and do the consistent work to achieve it. After all, the whole reason to set one is to change something—and that doesn't happen without thoughtful consistent execution. (Both "Cause and Effect" and "Ordinary Things, Consistently Done, Produce Extraordinary Results!" are full of related ideas to consider.)

Here it is on a bumper sticker: About the stupidest thing management can do is to announce some lofty goal for the year ("Our revenue target is $6,000,000 this year.") without any thought about the working plan to attain it. (In "It's Not About the Plan," I actually speak about the value of planning.)

Conventional wisdom and what actually works are often two

different things, and that is true for goal setting as well. Being aware of the most common misconceptions and goal setting mistakes will help you avoid these pitfalls and minimize the likelihood of sabotaging the attainment of your desired outcomes.

- The goal setter's focus is exclusively on the goal (Point B). Rarely is consideration given to the reality of where you are (Point A). How in the world can you get from here to there if you have no clue and haven't thought about where *here* is? Reality about here is critical to designing a path from here to there. In fact, one of the hardest parts of designing the journey is being sober about reality and painstakingly honest about your current situation. Psychiatric hospitals are filled with people who are delusional about reality.

- The goal is typically little more than wishful thinking. We don't like where we are and we wish it looked different; so, we chant the magic goal-setting words with the expectation that this psychobabble verbal wizardry will create the desired outcome, even though there is no specific path, metrics, or specific, executable plan to achieve it.

  Have you ever noticed that the vast majority of goals are glossy statements of a fantasy, not specific plans of action? The emphasis and focus is on the outcome and not the critical drivers or commitment required to achieve that outcome. By tracking your effort you will immediately know whether your goals are really goals or simply fantasies.

- The goal is not structured as a nonnegotiable but rather as a hope. We would all be better off if we had fewer goals and more standards. If the thing you want is important enough to set as a goal, why not make its attainment a nonnegotiable standard (a "must") instead of a desirable aspiration (a "should"—thank you, Tony Robbins). When you boil it down, a *should* means doing the best you can; a *must* means doing whatever it takes. Said a different way: You get what you tolerate.

- The vast majority of my goal-setting friends stumble at the beginning of the process because of a desire to dabble rather than burn the ships and commit. The emotional tug of continuing the search for an easier path or an early exit is hard to resist. My life works to the degree I keep my commitments.

- The goal setter rarely has accountability on either the execution of the critical drivers required to move toward the goal or the ultimate attainment of it. This explains why the typical goal setter makes the same goals year after year. No one to hold them accountable.

- Goal setters tend to fall in love with the goal instead of falling in love with the things that need to be done to accomplish the goal. In other words, they fall in love with the *effect* (goal) instead of the *cause* (critical drivers). If the critical driver for goal achievement were to want it bad enough or to visualize rays of sunshine emanating from your head, the human race would be rich, in a loving relationship and in great physical shape. They're not, so it isn't. (I discuss a similar issue in the chapter "Cause and Effect.")

- Often the goal setter compares her business to her friends' or competitors' to decide what goal to set, or she finds what's wrong and fantasizes about what the business would be like if she was there and not here. In other words, this type of goal setting makes where she is bad (wrong) and what she wants good (right). Being critical or judgmental about your current conditions is a guaranteed way to create massive unhappiness.

Let me quickly add that I am fully aware that fat and happy doesn't budge. Dissatisfaction or discomfort with where we are is a primary change agent in our lives. You will continue to sit in your chair in the exact same position until your body senses some discomfort, and then you will shift. What I am suggesting is that a dose of gratitude be injected into the process, because everything is not "bad." We all have a long list of things to be grateful for. Never say, "It can't get any worse," because it can get a lot worse. I love H. Ross Perot's definition of an entrepreneur: "Someone who is grateful for the progress that has been made and simultaneously dissatisfied with the rate they are making it."

- We know that having clarity on both Point A and Point B is critical to success. We also know that overcoming some obstacle that is preventing attainment of this outcome is fundamental to success. Clearly, progress cannot be made with wishful thinking; we need a specific plan. In the business world, the problem arises (particularly when a new project is being initiated) when the structure or form of the desired outcome becomes too rigid. This is a delicate dance and an easy place to trip yourself up. (Amazon has been particularly adept at walking this fine line with its willingness to invest, make mistakes, learn, and adjust to match the demand in the market. Read the "Day One" manifesto of founder and CEO Jeff Bezos.)

Here's the dance: The dreamer has a specific path planned and a specific form or structure that the outcome needs to look like when it is achieved. Being maniacally rigid about the ultimate vision (or path to achieve this vision), however, can obscure unplanned opportunities or alternate "forms" that might present themselves along the way but are not obvious because they are wrapped in a different skin than what was originally envisioned.

For example, we tend to ignore the unexpected good results that occur in our pursuit of the planned outcome and focus exclusively on the unexpected bad results (or problems). In the process, we spend all our time picking the weeds (which is necessary) and zero time watering our flowers (which is mandatory), much less even noticing them.

Another example might be that we start toward what we want and, in the process, the market tells us that what we have is interesting but what they want is something a little different.

The risk in being rigid is that the attachment to the original form will blind you to the seemingly unconnected random possibilities knocking on your door as you pursue the new thing.

- Bill and Jim figured this out. They started by selling candles door-to-door. The brothers-in-law (they married sisters) quickly found out, however, that even though the market thought candles were okay, what they really wanted was soap. Proctor & Gamble (Top 25 in the Fortune 500 rankings) was born from this willingness to listen closely to the market demand and shift strategies.

- Henry and Milton each had a similar epiphany when they approached the market with their grand schemes to be successful businessmen. Henry started his path to business success with vinegar. He failed, but in the process he found out what customers really wanted. He switched to tomato sauce. Milton started his career with caramel. The market was mildly interested (he later called it a fad), but he discovered that what they really wanted was chocolate. Henry Heinz made a fortune selling Heinz 57 ketchup, not vinegar. Milton Hershey killed it with the chocolate Hershey Kiss, not caramel.

In today's world, this kind of strategic/product shift is called a pivot. Figuring out where the original idea doesn't have legs and is struggling to get traction is one of the main benefits of taking the idea to the market. *Invention* happens in the laboratory. *Innovation* happens by engaging with the market.

Here it is on a bumper sticker: Don't let your obsession with the dream get in the way of noticing the demand. Or as my friends on Wall Street say, "When the duck quacks, feed it."

The market really doesn't care what you want to give it, nor does it care how much you love what you have created. The market wants a problem solved or a gap filled. When they tell you what that is, create that! (See both "Mommas Love Their Babies" and "O Baby!" for practical guidelines about attracting and retaining customers.)

The balance between the founder's dreams and the market's demand is delicate because abandoning the dream prematurely to pursue the next new shiny penny is dumb. Most things take longer to accomplish than originally estimated. On the other hand, hanging on long after the fat lady has cleared her throat is suicidal.

The key is to be aware of opportunities that present themselves along the way which might not look the way you originally envisioned but are a superior path from here to there.

Most exceptionally successful people probably ended up in the vicinity of where they thought they were going, but the path (or product) that got them there was circuitous. They achieved their success by remaining nimble, inquisitive, and responsive to the opportunities that came their way even when those opportunities were not what they expected (or originally planned).

Take a look at where you are in your life today. Chances are these three things are true:

1. Where you are today is beyond your wildest dreams compared to what you thought was possible when you were eighteen years old.

2. The route you took to get here was totally unpredictable from your vantage point as an eighteen-year-old.

3. The path that got you here was anything but linear or planned. If your life even remotely resembles mine, your path to this point is the most convoluted and tortuous route imaginable. Yet, here I am!

How did you get here? It certainly wasn't massive expertise in goal setting, as important as that might be to you. It was a willingness to create, engage with the market, learn from your mistakes, and be responsive to opportunities after the journey started vs. obsessively grinding on the original dream. It was allowing for the possibility of something different from the original form you envisioned.

Thinking Time

- When I think about the outcomes (goals) we have set for the coming quarter or year, where do I need to get clarity about my starting point in terms of environment, resources, competition, etc.?

- Who can I ask to help me think through our reality so that I minimize the likelihood of tricking myself about our starting point or current capabilities?
- What is the specific path/plan we have designed to move us from here to there, and what additional color or specificity do I need to add to this path to make it executable?
- What would it take to transition our plans from "shoulds" (wouldn't it be nice if . . .) to "musts" (failure is not an option)?
- What are the hard decisions and actions I have been postponing in the irrational hope I can "goal" it away?
- What are the nonnegotiable standards we must establish?
- What am I tolerating in my business that is sabotaging my results or that is incongruent with my standards?
- How do we build in the accountability required for the critical driver standards and outcomes we have committed to achieving?
- What is the specificity I need to add to our plan so that everyone on the team has a clear, measurable metric (target) they are shooting for?
- What are the specific causes I must identify that will enable the effect I want to happen?
- What have we done well and what am I grateful for?
- What are the unexpected opportunities that are being presented that might move us in the direction we want but don't look the way we thought they would look? (Where is there a gaggle of quacking ducks?)

NOW . . . Go Think! You will thank me later.
KJC

CHAPTER 17

THE BIG 8

Leaders inspire . . . Managers control. To be successful in business, we need both.

Unfortunately, most senior management teams and business owners spend the majority of their time reacting to the urgent and babysitting (begging) employees and, therefore, have very little available bandwidth for inspiring and leading. Interestingly, the thing business owners spend the majority of their time trying to do (controlling) is the least enjoyable activity for both the Owner and the "controlled" employee.

The Big 8 process does all the heavy "control" lifting for you. It's a method to control the process without trying to control the people. The Big 8 process is sequential. For example, it does no good to create a plan without clarity on either the outcome or the obstacle, and for sure there is no ability to understand who should be on the team or how to measure them without the plan.

The key to effective "management" is clarity on the design, communication, and implementation of the components of the Big 8 process. The Big 8 is a series of progressive steps that shifts the organization from high maintenance to high performance and significantly reduces the time and effort required to "manage." With the Big 8, your employees own their jobs and are accountable for their outcomes!

The Big 8 has two sections: "What" and "How." Extreme clarity around each is critical to successful implementation of the Big 8 process.

What

1. The specific measurable outcomes (or standards) you—as Owner/CEO/leader—have prioritized for the business.

2. The primary obstacle that is prohibiting the forward progress from Point A (where you are) to Point B (where you would like to be). Clarity on this "gap" is critical to understanding the problem and converting the problem into an opportunity. (Refresh your memory about Core Discipline #2—Separate the Problem from the Symptom by rereading "The 5 Core Disciplines of Thinking" at the beginning of the book.)

How

3. The plan or strategy your team has created (with your adult supervision and input) to overcome this obstacle. The plan will also describe the resources required to execute the plan as well as the timelines, including milestones (interim targets) and delivery dates.

4. The process, machine, tactics, tasks, and executables required to put rubber on the road and to make actual sustainable progress. The key is identifying the specific resources, skills, training, processes, systems, equipment, best practices, and operations required to drive results.

5. The team of A players who have a high internal, emotional need to succeed, the requisite execution intelligence (been there, done that), and a scorecard to set performance standards of excellence. (Sweat, long hours, good intentions, likability, loyalty, and tenure are sorry excuses for results and equally pathetic benchmarks for

employee evaluation and compensation.) Without an individual scorecard that clearly outlines the deliverables required to earn an A, how can you possibly grade or coach each player's performance? (Read the CEO-centric chapter "A CEO Should *Never* Delegate . . ." for a complementary take on this Big 8 topic.)

6. The critical drivers and standards that must be executed, measured, and analyzed to ensure the accurate and timely delivery of the outcomes. Critical drivers are the "causes" that, when consistently executed, produce the desired "effects." (Take a look at the "Cause and Effect" chapter for more insights about critical drivers and outcomes.)

7. The great dashboards that display your critical driver results in a format that allows you and your team to have immediate optics. Regular comparison of the actual critical driver results produced against the benchmark standards established (and the trend line of these results) is critical to understanding where the opportunities are to adjust and correct the execution.

    Without a dashboard, you get a story. Dashboards tell you what you need to know, not what you want to believe. Regular analysis is mandatory to establish reasons for the progress (or lack thereof) toward the stated outcomes and benchmark standards. Without the analysis, we have more data and information, but no knowledge about what to do differently.

    As one of my mentors told me forty-five years ago: "Keith, there is hope and there are facts. When they collide, facts win every time." Or, as my friends in Dubai keep reminding me, "Believe in Allah, but tie up your camel."

8. The regular, candid (sometimes difficult, many times complimentary) accountability and coaching conversations with the team members to make the necessary corrections and adjustments.

    Without coaching and consequences, good intentions and "the best I can" will become the excuse du jour. Without coaching and consequences, critical drivers and outcomes will become suggestions, not standards. (The firsthand example I include in "Help Me Understand" illustrates this vividly.)

The Big 8 is by far the most powerful tool in my business tool belt for creating clarity, ownership, accountability, and consistency with my team. This process is designed to be *the* primary control and accountability tool for the outcomes we have prioritized . . . which frees me up to lead. The Big 8 process (which dovetails nicely with the "A CEO Should *Never* Delegate . . ." chapter) is the key to transitioning from Operator to Owner.

As the leader of the business, you are primary on the "What" portion of this process (items 1 and 2). The business needs you to determine the outcomes and obstacles. The beauty of the Big 8 is that your team is primary on the "How" (items 3 through 7). Your employees are responsible for creating the plan that drives the organization from here to there.

If they create the plan, it's *their* plan and they *own* it. If they understand the definition of an A player, they own their performance in comparison with that standard.

If the team is primary on establishing the critical drivers and standards required to meet your outcomes, and they design the dashboards that provide optics on the team's performance, they own that too.

One of the stupidest things management can do is dictate the plan on how something is going to be accomplished. Not only does a top-down approach destroy the basic human need for autonomy and self-direction, it erodes ownership, innovation, and engagement. I am not encouraging you to abdicate or create a free-for-all environment. Your oversight, input, and adult supervision are critical in the plan creation process, but so are your employees and team members. (This relates seamlessly with your role in creating the corporate culture, so I encourage you to read the chapter "Culture Is King (You Get What You Tolerate)" as well.)

Here it is on a bumper sticker: If they create it, they own it.

As the leader of the organization, you reenter the process and are primary on the coaching conversations (item 8). Great coaches guide, encourage, and teach. But the greatest coaches have the courage to create a culture of discipline and outcomes, which is why great coaches are always revered by their players. I love the U.S. Marine Corps slogan: "If you want the most, make it easy. If you want the best, make it hard."

As you implement the Big 8, you will find two points where leverage is created:

- the machine that gets designed and built
- the people operating the machine

The better or more robust the machine, the more sustainable the progress in overcoming the obstacles. The better the team who design and operate the machine, the greater the efficiency and operational excellence (results). Getting the machine and the people right are critical to performance, optimization, and hitting the desired outcomes.

A word of caution: Missing any one of these steps is a prescription for slipping back into the time-consuming role of reacting, begging, and controlling. In other words, tired. You cannot babysit your way to high performance and accountability.

The Thinking Time possibilities for The Big 8 are larger than usual (and will take multiple sessions to work through), but the juice is definitely worth the squeeze. Do the work, get the results. You will be happy you did (so will your bank account)!

Thinking Time
General
- Where (exactly) have we fallen short on the Big 8 and what (exactly) do I need to do to create the accountability and culture of high performance?
- When I honestly evaluate our current progress, how much of my frustration is attributable to a miss on the Big 8 process? Where are the misses and what needs to be done now?

Outcomes

- What are the few specific measurable outcomes I am optimizing for? (The clear, measurable target on the wall.)
- What are the specific expectations I have about what these outcomes look like when they are achieved? (What does success look like . . . specifically?)
- How do I successfully communicate these outcomes and create 100% clarity with my team about my expectations?

Primary Gap/Obstacle

- What is the primary obstacle that is impeding our progress between Point A and Point B?
- If this obstacle is so obvious, why haven't we seen or addressed this obstacle previously? (Is this really the obstacle or is it a symptom disguising the real problem?)
- What sacrifices will we need to make or risks we will need to take to overcome this obstacle?
- By saying "yes" to solving this obstacle, what are we required to say "no" to?
- If we are to be successful in overcoming this obstacle, what must we start doing and what must we stop doing?
- What is the specific measurable gap between where I am and where I want to be?

Strategy/Plan

- What is the specific plan that will serve as our road map and guide on closing the gap so that we always know where we are in relation to the desired outcomes and have clarity on what needs to be executed and corrected?
- What are the specific measurable tasks that need to be performed to deliver these outcomes?
- Who will perform these tasks?

- What are the skill sets and execution intelligence required to perform these tasks?
- What are the resources (time, money, and people) required to successfully execute this plan? (See the "Options Analysis Matrix" chapter for clarity about allocating resources.)
- What is the projected outcome and specific target date for completion?
- What are the interim milestones (dates and progress points) that will tell me if we are on track for hitting the completion deadline?
- What is my strategy to overcome the primary obstacle in our way?

Machine

- What are the specific processes, tactics, tasks, executables, and resources required for something to actually get done?
- What are the skills, physical and personnel assets, training, and best practices required to successfully build this machine and keep it running?
- What is the sequence of events that will ensure that we build this machine in the correct order?

A Players

- What is the scorecard I have created for each person on the team? Without a scorecard to proactively measure and grade results and specific deliverables against a benchmark/standard, I have no ability to either grade or coach performance. (See Appendix 3 for an example of a CEO scorecard.)
- In evaluating my current team, where have I settled and, therefore, produced mediocrity?
- When I really look at the quality, capability, and performance of the people I have on my team, where is there an opportunity to reset expectations, train, upgrade, or replace?

- Knowing what I now know, are there any people on my current team that I would not rehire . . . and what am I prepared to do about it? (Where are the weak links?)
- What can I do to upgrade the quality of my choices for enhancing the number of A players on my team?
- Since the team I have represents the vast majority of the leverage I enjoy, what needs to be done to guarantee their success?
- Is part of the problem with my team a reflection of the culture I have created or tolerated? What are the changes I must make to our culture and how am I going to do that? (See both "Culture Is King (You Get What You Tolerate)" and "The Apology" for practical guidance on this topic.)

Critical Drivers

- I know that what gets measured is what gets managed, so what are the three to five critical activities that must be performed and measured on a regular basis to ensure significant progress toward my standards and outcomes? (The chapter "Cause and Effect" will be extremely useful for you to reread in thinking about critical drivers.)
- What are the specific measurable standards of performance I have for each critical driver activity?
- I know that anyone who doesn't want to measure doesn't want to be held accountable, so what accountability metrics do I need to establish to assess our actual performance against our standards?

Dashboards/Measuring

- Under the heading of transforming data into usable information that can be analyzed and provide me with valuable optics, what dashboard or scoreboard do I need to create and monitor so that I can easily see our progress on executing the critical drivers as well as achievement of our overall outcomes?

- What dashboard would I need to create so that my team can look at it and know exactly where performance is deteriorating from prior time periods or in comparison to the standard?
- Information is simply data that has been organized, which is the role of a dashboard. I need knowledge, not more information. The key to knowledge is analysis of the information. When I look at my dashboards, what are the insights and distinctions I can glean about our execution and performance in comparison to the standards we have set and outcomes we have prioritized?
- What critical or interdependent relationships do I need to analyze to be able to see what is actually happening to sabotage our results?
- Based on this analysis, what course corrections are needed?

Coaching/Consequences

- Under the theory that nothing can change until the unsaid is spoken, what are the hard conversations I know I need to have but have avoided in my misguided desire to keep the peace or minimize the disruption of the status quo?
- Where have I lowered my standards and tolerated mediocrity in my team's performance?
- Who needs the hard coaching and reset on expectations for deliverables or culture?
- What are the clear consequences for missing the standards and outcomes we have set?
- Since my employees do not need to beg for their paychecks, why do I constantly find myself begging them to do their job, and what do I need to do about this problem?
- What can I do to consistently communicate my appreciation and acknowledgment for a job well done?

NOW . . . Go Think! You will thank me later.
KJC

CHAPTER 18

SOMETHING FOR NOTHING . . . *SERIOUSLY?*

The single most powerful force I have in my life is the words that I use to describe my situation. The reason? *The label becomes the experience.* Said another way, the dog becomes yours when you name it.

If I lose a ton of money in a deal, I might be tempted to say, "This is a catastrophe," and therefore my experience will be a disaster of cataclysmic proportions. If, on the other hand, I lose the same ton of money and I say, "Now this is going to be challenging," my experience will be challenging. The experience has not changed, only the label. By changing the label, I change my experience.

Too often we hear or use words and labels without really thinking about how these words will impact our experience, or even if they are meaningful. For example, one of the most popular concepts in the world of half-baked financial entertainment is "passive income."

Think about the word "passive," which *Webster's* defines as "inactive." So the concept being peddled is creating income by doing nothing. In reality, the concept being pushed is "doing the least to get the most."

Passive income makes about as much sense as passive health or passive relationships. You would scoff at the idea of a passive weight loss technique or a passive gold medal in the Olympics or a passive marriage.

But financial shamans write hundreds of these books every year counting on you to lurch to the door marked "Something for Nothing." (See "Mmm . . . Kool-Aid" for more Thinking Time ideas on this topic.) But somehow this concept of passive income has gotten traction. (Here is a pretty good rule of thumb: Never buy anything from someone who is out of breath.)

Visualize a merry-go-round the size of a football stadium, for example. Suppose 2,000 people jumped onto the merry-go-round and started begging you to push them. You start to push, but the merry-go round is so heavy it doesn't budge. You are straining and pushing with all your might. Your muscles start to quiver, and sweat is pouring from your brow. You don't think it will ever move. Finally, after a long time of intense effort, you sense the slightest movement, which causes you to redouble your intensity. You continue to strain and push and sweat . . . and the merry-go-round picks up speed. The faster it goes, the less effort it takes to keep it going. You keep pushing, and when the merry-go-round is really turning, you stop pushing, put your hands in your pockets, and go "passive." What happens to the merry-go-round? It stops, of course.

There is nothing passive about getting the merry-go-round going and there is certainly nothing passive about keeping it going. *Everything requires effort and maintenance.* There is no passive path to success at anything, especially finances and wealth.

What is required to keep the merry-go-round moving is an occasional swoop with your hand against one of the handlebars. Swooping your hand against the handlebars is NOT passive, but it is leverage—and I'm a huge believer in leveraged income.

The distinction I'm making is this: Passive anything is a bad idea and ultimately unworkable because it requires us to fall into the trap of thinking there is a way to do nothing and still get what we want or to maintain what we have by being inactive. No part of your life or business works that way.

When you stop to really look at the most financially successful people on the planet—Bill Gates, Michael Dell, Oprah Winfrey, Richard

Branson, George Soros, Larry Ellison, or anyone else you can think of—you will not find a single one of them who either got rich or is staying rich by being inactive or doing the least. In fact, they will all tell you that keeping their money requires at least as much work as was exerted in making it in the first place. They are all active. They are all engaged and involved. And, they are leveraged. Furthermore, not one of them started their businesses based on the Kool-Aid of passive income. If they had, they would have done nothing.

Thinking Time

- Where am I looking for the path of doing the least or the door marked "something for nothing" to create the success I want?
- Under the banner of doing the work required to deserve the success I desire, what needs to be done?
- To achieve the success I desire, what effort and expertise are required?
- Where are the sources of leverage I can capitalize on that would increase my production, revenue, or profits?
- What do I need to learn, or who do I need to hire, to help us create and sustain the profitability we are capable of producing?
- When I look at my competitors who are bigger and better than I am, what leverage did they create or what resources were acquired to attain that level of success?
- What have we done in the past that worked?
- What ideas have we had in the past that we didn't follow through on?
- What ideas have we had in the past where we dabbled and didn't fully commit or didn't execute with enough intensity or consistency?
- What have I been procrastinating on doing that would help us get traction on this project?
- Where have I been active but not productive?

- What leverage do I need to enable me to create better results by utilizing someone else's time, money, brains, network, or skills?
- Where do we need to improve our execution so that we are more competitive in the marketplace?

NOW . . . Go Think! You will thank me later.

KJC

CHAPTER 19

THE ONLY CONSTANT IN BUSINESS IS . . .

Albert Einstein gave his students at Princeton the exact same final exam every semester for twenty years. After just a couple of years, his students figured out the predictability of the questions, and so did his fellow professors. One of his peers asked him why he continued to use the same final exam questions year after year. Albert's reply? "Because the answers keep on changing." He was so smart!

The only constant in business is change. A good idea three years ago could be a bad idea today. A great idea today could be a disaster next quarter. The answers I have now were answers created in a different environment at a different time. (For much more on this topic, see "The Advantage of Being Small" and "The Bathrobe Theory of Business: When a Good Idea Isn't.")

Look no further than how tens of thousands of people made millions between 1996 and 2000. They woke up every morning, turned on CNBC, and bought every dot-com listed on the NASDAQ stock exchange. Or how lots of these same people made millions more by buying and flipping single-family homes in Las Vegas between 2002 and 2007. Like all great ideas, these were seemingly brilliant (and bulletproof) until they weren't. What caused them to go from being a great idea to a horrible one? A change in the environment.

Here it is on a bumper sticker: The reason companies lose relevance, go broke, or fade into the sunset is because they continue to grow, but fail to evolve. They rely on the wrong questions and old answers. Great questions, an open mind, flexibility, and a healthy dose of paranoia are your best friends in business. No business is safe: 435 of the Fortune 500 (87%) from 1955 are now gone . . . disappeared . . . kaput. The business environment kept on changing—requiring a different set of answers—and they didn't come up with a better question. Stupid!

Thinking Time

- Where has the environment in which we've been operating (economic, technology, regulatory, competition, customer preferences, employees, cultural) changed over the last few years?
- How are customers' expectations different today than they were two or five years ago?
- What will customers' expectations be twelve months from now?
- Where has our expertise (relevance) as a company lagged or stagnated in the last thirty-six months?
- What skills or personnel do we need to add to excel at what we do, shift our direction, and optimize our bottom line?
- What is happening competitively that could change what we sell, how it is sold, the price we charge, and where/how/what we message?
- Are we learning, training, and evolving as fast as things are changing?
- Based on the answer to the questions above, what do we need to learn, who do we need to hire, what do we need to change to remain relevant and competitive?

NOW . . . Go Think! You will thank me later.
KJC

P.S. Eastman Kodak, AOL, Yahoo!, Sears, Myspace, and Radio Shack all wish they had heard this advice!

CHAPTER 20

EVERYTHING COUNTS

A couple of years ago Sandi and I wanted some golfing downtime, which we do several times each year to escape the Texas heat. We found a five-star golf resort in California that looked promising, so we booked our ten-day trip of golf, massages, and R&R.

Below are excerpts from a letter I wrote to the manager of the resort after returning home from our vacation.

Dear Ms. Harper,

Sandi and I recently stayed in one of your suites at the Majestic Resort . . . a beautiful property with a superb golf course. I will suggest to you that based on the quality of food and service, your 5 Star rating is in serious jeopardy.

One evening we ate at your fine dining restaurant (once was enough), and the food was not edible. Our steaks had literally been microwaved and tasted like it. (Our waiter verified the microwave part of this disastrous meal.)

The grill at the golf clubhouse was our venue for breakfast every morning. And every day for ten straight days we sent our food back to the kitchen for one reason or another (mostly because the eggs were cold, the bacon undercooked, the English muffins not toasted, or the coffee not hot).

Now here is the really interesting part of this ordeal. It got to where we were warning our waiter of the issues we had experienced on previous mornings before *we ordered so that those same mistakes could be avoided. Our warnings were useless. The eggs still came out cold, the bacon undercooked . . . not once, not twice, but* every single morning for ten straight days! *If it wasn't costing us so much money, it would have been hilarious as a skit on* Saturday Night Live.

Should you be thinking the Cunninghams are crazy people for continuing to go back to a restaurant that clearly is incapable of solving these problems, I can assure you that if there had been a different on-site alternative, we would have gladly stopped banging our forehead on this wall. Alas, no alternatives and hope springs eternal.

As an Owner of multiple businesses, I know Yelp does not fix problems, but it does make the "yelper" feel significant and heard. But I happen to believe there's a better way to fix these kinds of problems than broadcasting an opinion over the internet, which is why I am writing you this letter.

When I see this kind of poor performance on a consistent basis—at a luxury resort, no less!—it can only be a result of one of four things:

1. *Incompetent and uncaring employees (This is a hiring and culture issue.)*
2. *A lack of training*
3. *No measurements or accountability*
4. *A lack of supervision*

In the case of the Majestic, I suspect it is all four. (As my friends in the pest control business remind me, "There is always more than one cockroach in the kitchen. If you see one, it is only a matter of time before you meet his relatives." I agree. I think we met all the cousins on this trip.)

I know this kind of stuff can happen but it does not happen when the owners and management team are committed to a great hiring process, creating an excellent culture, training and retraining, measuring, and accountability.

While it might be tempting to place the blame on the kitchen staff, the cook, or the waiter, all these people (and how they perform their job) are a reflection on the Majestic management team and not the individuals who are delivering the crappy service.

I also know that it is unlikely that you and your leadership team are aware of these issues; otherwise, they would have been addressed. My experience is that all owners and senior management teams give lip service to the concept of having happy customers and guests, but often they are unaware of the quality of service being delivered. (Probably no one at the top has bothered to leave their office in the last couple of months.) If that is the case here, then consider this your wake-up call to address your management team and culture issues.

The fact that I have taken the time to write this letter should indicate to you the degree of my disappointment about the expectations you set and the service you actually delivered. I had such high hopes that Majestic would become a regular destination for our golf getaways.

Based on this experience, however, our search continues for a 5 Star golf resort that offers great weather, great golf, great accommodations, great service, and great food. Failing at 1 out of 5, when a 5 is promised, is not a 5. It's a 0 because we won't come back.

Sincerely,

Keith J. Cunningham

About ten days after I emailed this letter, I received an email reply from Ms. Harper's administrative assistant in which she suggested a specific time when it would be convenient for Ms. Harper to speak with me. My own email reply to Ms. Harper's helper was short and sweet.

No need to bother Ms. Harper, since the issues I raised were obviously not significant enough to warrant a direct response from her. Let her know that having her admin people reach out to me is an indication that she is not taking me or my problems seriously. I suspect that if my last name was Dell or Gates or Buffett I would have heard directly from her, and it would not have taken ten days to get a response. Furthermore, she would have wanted to know what time would be convenient for me to take a call from her, not the other way around. Please let her know she has thrown gasoline onto the fire.

Two weeks later (twenty-five days after the first letter), Ms. Harper managed to clear her calendar long enough to reach out me to directly. She listened patiently as I recounted my story, mumbled the appropriate institutionalized apology, and then delivered the coup de grâce: "Mr. Cunningham, please let us know if you intend to stay with us again so that we can upgrade your room and provide you with a complimentary round of golf."

WTF! Are you serious? I couldn't believe I was hearing this!

I concluded the call with:

Ms. Harper, the problem happened this *time, not next time. I paid for something I didn't get* this *time, and the reason I didn't get it is because the management and staff at the Majestic resort are incompetent.*

A discount for future services as compensation for poor performance on past services is analogous to getting salmonella at a restaurant and the restaurant owner offering me a free dessert the next time I eat there. I already got sick from this ill-conceived trip, and your idea of helping me get over the food poisoning is to offer a token discount on my next trip?

I have taken enough of my time to try to help you. Please let me know if you ever leave the Majestic for another property so that we can avoid accidentally experiencing this level of service again.

Where is my password to Yelp?

Thinking Time

- In the last year, how many people tried us and never came back?
- How much did that lack of repeat business cost us in incremental revenue and profitability?
- If everything counts and nothing is neutral, where are we missing the mark on delivering on our promise and meeting our customers' expectations?
- How can I be certain that our team is performing to our standards?
- How can I make sure we are consistently executing and meeting our customers' expectations?
- What is our commitment to training and how can I be sure the training we offer is getting the traction and implementation I expect?
- What can cause our customers to not come back and what are we doing as a management team to prevent customer defection?
- What can we do to get the honest assessment from our customers about their experience so that we can minimize the likelihood of a customer firing us because of substandard performance?
- What are our "cold eggs and untoasted English muffin" that are sabotaging our customers' experience?

NOW . . . Go Think! You will thank me later.
KJC

CHAPTER 21

THE 3 PILLARS OF SUCCESS

I hate short lists that attempt to jam all the ingredients for success into a pithy little formula. Success and mastery are far more complex than pith. Having said this, however, let me give you some cogent advice about making consistent, measurable progress toward your outcomes.

If you will do these three things on a regular (daily) basis for ninety days, you will be stunned at the progress you will achieve.

1. **Write down your major outcomes every day.** You will notice I did not use the word "goals." In our culture, a goal has become synonymous with a wish. "I wish my profits were \$10,000/month higher. Oh, I'll make that my new goal." I do not think we need to get better at goal setting. I think we need to get better at setting nonnegotiable standards. (Turn to "Dreams and Demand" for much more about the foolishness of having goals without a plan and the concurrent commitment to do the necessary work to achieve them.) Writing and rewriting your most significant outcomes (major objectives, not "To Do" list items) forces you to *focus* on the most critical things that need to be worked on and accomplished. It's a tragedy to major in minor things.

2. **Plan your day before it starts.** This simply means you sit down

with your calendar and think about the most critical action items you must knock out today. Make sure your calendar reflects your priorities every day. Progress is not built by doing something huge but rather by consistently doing ordinary things. (This is so deeply ingrained in my thinking that I've devoted an entire chapter to it called "Ordinary Things, Consistently Done, Produce Extraordinary Results!")

3. **Be accountable to someone for your plans, commitments, and results.** Here is the truth: Our brains are simply too powerful at making excuses and creating elaborate justifications for why we did not get something important done or did not follow through on a task. We make promises to ourselves, but we break them with alarming regularity. For some reason, promises we make to ourselves are less sacred than the promises we make to others. Having an accountability partner who will hold you to your commitments is a key ingredient to making sustainable progress and for success. Someone who will tell you the truth; someone who will not buy into your cheap excuses for why you fell off the wagon or didn't get the job done; someone to tell you "no."

Here it is on a bumper sticker: The higher you go or the better you want to get, the greater the requirement to have someone in your life who will hold you accountable and tell you the truth.

Thinking Time

- What are the one or two major outcomes and deliverables I am prepared to commit to achieving this quarter? This year?
- What are the business outcomes and results I am prepared to make nonnegotiable?
- What would prevent me from finding an extra five minutes every morning (before I turn on my computer) to write down my major outcomes and plan my day before it starts? How could I create a ritual for this so that I didn't miss for ninety days?

- What are the specific priorities and executables I must focus on and get on my calendar to create the momentum and results I have planned?
- I know that guardrails and rules help me avoid feeding every kitty scratching at my screen door. What are the most frequent reasons my calendar gets hijacked, and what guardrails do I need to build to keep these intruders from sabotaging my day?
- Who have I given permission to tell me the truth and hold me accountable?
- How frequently will I check in with this person?
- Am I willing to tell this person the truth so that he has the opportunity to coach me?
- Am I ready to play this game to win, or do I want to keep dabbling . . . hoping to get lucky? What does that look like, specifically?

NOW . . . Go Think! You will thank me later.
KJC

CHAPTER 22

THE ADVANTAGE
OF BEING SMALL

The big guys seem to have all the advantages. Resources? Money? The biggest companies in the world have tons of resources and seemingly bottomless pits of money. People? They can hire the best and the brightest, pay signing bonuses, issue stock options galore, cut enormous paychecks, and provide outrageous perks. Marketing presence? The big guys have the brand, reputation, a marketing machine, and momentum most of us are dying to achieve. They also have legacy costs, expensive infrastructure, and a bias for protecting the status quo, which makes change very difficult, painful, and unpopular.

The only things "small" has going for it are flexibility and intimacy of relationships.

Small should be able to turn on a dime. What creates opportunity for the small guys (the entrepreneurs of the world) is the *inflexibility* of the big guys to treat each customer as a king (instead of a transaction) and every employee as a queen (instead of just another nameless cog in the machine).

It is the smaller players in the market that are driving change and taking advantage of evolving customer preferences, innovative ideas, pathetic customer service, and emerging trends that the bigger players cannot see, don't care about, or cannot respond to fast enough.

Charles Darwin is famous for his theory of "survival of the fittest." What is particularly interesting is his definition of the word "fittest." He did not conclude that it was the biggest, fastest, strongest, richest, oldest, or smartest. He hypothesized that it is the most adaptable.

It turns out that the key to survival in the business world is how flexible you are in response to changes in the marketplace or the environment. A strategy of changing your environment to improve your situation is doomed.

Size is frequently the enemy of flexibility, handicapping your ability to adapt and change. Sears, BlackBerry, Blockbuster, Woolworth's, and the entire newspaper publishing industry are proof that your prior success means nothing when the environment changes.

Hubris and faulty assumptions killed every one of them.

Here it is on a bumper sticker: Survival requires more curiosity and less arrogance; more humility and less need to be right; better questions and fewer answers.

Flexibility requires an acute awareness of where you are in relation to the environment: What is shifting around you and what is or isn't working? This is why I am such a fanatic about measuring and optics. How in the world can you see stuff changing if you are not measuring it?

Small succeeds because it has so little to lose, embraces mistakes, and is committed to learning. Small is willing to experiment and fail. Big succeeds by brute force, dogma, erecting barriers, and institutionalizing and systematizing success.

Be careful, though. Small destroys its only competitive advantage by attempting to emulate the big guys when it comes to these areas:

- **Establish committees**—The unwilling appoint the unfit to do the unnecessary.

- **Govern by consensus**—Always produces mediocrity.

- **Create standardized systems to ensure compliance and uniformity**—Drains excitement and flexibility. ("Systems vs. Flexibility" has lots on this topic if you're interested—and you should be.)

- **Abdicate decision making to accommodate the lowest common denominator**—Compromise is the enemy of excellence.

- **Optimize for safe and no ripples**—Promotes the status quo.

- **Attempt to grow by casually pleasing the masses instead of deeply pleasing the niche**—Homogenizes your product, service, and brand to the point they will be indistinguishable from everyone else's.

- **Design "paint by number," standardized, year-end annual employee evaluations forms and processes**—Misses the point of coaching the performance and potential of your employees.

- **Allow HR to decide whom we hire and how we onboard, communicate, manage, compensate, and lead our employees**—Institutionalizes the relationship by turning employees into cogs in a machine.

- **Optimize for standardization**—Forfeits relationships and intimacy.

- **Lower standards out of fear of hurting someone's feelings**—Destroys culture and creates mediocrity.

I am not saying committees, standardization, and systems are not useful. I have a process for how I go about packing for a trip. I also have a routine I go through when I exercise and a system for how I organize the accounting and reporting procedures for our various business interests.

Systems, procedures, and policies help us cope with life. Without them, every day is a brand-new day and things would take forever to get done.

But, this desire to get big by cloning what big does is frequently counterproductive and costly. If you don't yet have the brute force of size, abandoning the advantages of small is stupid. (Reading "*Everything Counts*" will help you avoid stupid.)

Thinking Time

- Where have I allowed my business to abandon the advantages of being small?
- Where have I encouraged/tolerated systems and standardization as a substitute for intimacy and relationship?
- Where could I inject some flexibility back into how we are doing business?
- Where do I sense a shift in the market that I have been afraid to investigate because of an irrational fear that it might disrupt what we are currently doing?
- What are the things we should be doing if I weren't so afraid of losing?
- How can I test these ideas in a small way so that in case it is a bad idea, it doesn't torpedo the mother ship?
- What assumptions am I making about the current environment and my competition that, if wrong, would cause me significant economic distress?
- What is the competitive advantage we have relied on to attract and retain customers? What could erode or undermine this advantage?
- Knowing what I know about my business, if I decided to compete with myself, what would I do to put a major dent in my company?
- Where am I hanging on to strategies and solutions that were great answers in a different environment?
- What question do I need to ask to discover our vulnerability to a changing environment?
- What do we need to measure to have optics about what is changing?

NOW . . . Go Think! You will thank me later.

KJC

CHAPTER 23

SIMPLIFYING GROWTH

As business owners, we are always on the prowl for more customers, more growth, and more revenue. Unfortunately, this quest usually begins and ends with a tactical solution.

When we look at the top-line revenue, we tend to say things like:

- *Our biggest problem is not enough people know about us.*

- *In order to grow, I need to increase the size of my lead-gen funnel.*

- *If I only had a Biz Dev person to help me stir up leads.*

- *We need to be on page one of Google.*

- *I need to hire two new salespeople.*

- *We should offer a special promotion or installation discount to help us attract new customers.*

These are all *tactical* solutions. But it is always a mistake to start your thinking with tactical. Tactical sounds like, "What could we do to increase sales?" Strategic sounds like, "Why are our sales numbers not twice as big? What is the core obstacle preventing the doubling of our revenue?" Asking a tactical question will always result in tactical answers. Solving the problem that isn't, however, is a waste of time and money.

(This idea is so crucial it's my Core Discipline of Thinking #2 and a key focus in the chapter "Strategic Growth.")

The reason we gravitate to a tactical answer is because we are hard-wired to get busy . . . to do something . . . to take action. The illusion we live with is that being active is synonymous with being productive. Dumb!

The key is to start with four really simple questions (I've made them this chapter's Thinking Time topics) to get you thinking about growth in a more productive way. Once the strategic part is handled, the tactics become easier to prioritize and the results will speak for themselves.

Thinking Time

- Who do I want to buy from me?
- What must happen to cause them to buy?
- What must happen to keep them coming back?
- What could happen to cause them not to buy?

NOW . . . Go Think! You will thank me later.
KJC

P.S. If you spend less than ten hours on these four questions, you have missed the point!

CHAPTER 24

THE BATHROBE THEORY OF BUSINESS: WHEN A GOOD IDEA ISN'T

Although it seems obvious when you think about it, a good idea for me might be a horrible idea for you. A good investment opportunity for Richard Branson could be a horrible investment for me. A great idea a year ago is likely to be a fatal idea today, yet we still look to other people and other times to filter and grade our ideas.

In our desire for certainty, a map, and familiar landmarks, we tend to look for patterns that will tell us a story and provide an illusion of safety. An inability or unwillingness to distinguish between the story and the facts, however, has caused more than a few bankruptcies. Enamored by the story, we fail to take into consideration the changes in the environment or our lack of skills to actually execute on the "good" idea being promoted or the risk characteristics inherent in choosing solution A vs. solution B. Make the problem the problem, not the story. You can't fix a story. (If you're reading this book sequentially, go back and reread "The Only Constant in Business Is . . .".)

Rest assured, the number of websites that get rebuilt or SEO initiatives that get launched has more to do with consultants who are experts at selling and the urban legend of what "works" than they do with an actual problem that requires attention.

The question I frequently ask is, "Does the solution I have solve the problem I've got?" Problem solving tends to be 80% discovery and diagnostics. (Both the chapter "Generalizations Kill Clarity" and the description of Core Discipline #2—Separate the Problem from the Symptom in "The 5 Core Disciplines of Thinking" address this issue.)

One of our Board members, who was frustrated by the lack of acceleration in her revenue (sales were "only" climbing at 35% instead of her desired 50%), showed up for a quarterly Board meeting with a branding proposal from a marketing expert she had met the prior month at an industry seminar. The proposal was for a total new look, color scheme, website, collateral material, tagline, font, messaging, and logo. The cost was a smooth $300,000.

My question to this incredibly bright entrepreneur was: Do you think potential customers are now clicking on your website, seeing your font size, logo, and color scheme and saying to themselves, "Wow, I really like what these guys are offering and it really does solve my problem better than anything else I have seen; the price is great and I think this will work for us. But . . . Nope, I'm not going to buy from these guys . . . wrong font size."

With more discussion and advice from her Board over the next thirty minutes, she was able to identify several key issues that were probably closer to being the problem than the logo and font. She spent $35,000 on fixing the real problem and achieved a 46% bump in revenue over the next twelve months.

Now, I am not opposed to any of these branding tactics, font size changes, or website solutions. There are times when any or all of them might be critically important, but getting sold or relying on the crowd is very different from understanding the problem and choosing what to buy to help you solve the problem that is.

Here it is on a bumper sticker: Business is not a bathrobe. One size does not fit all. Different problems in different environments for different people at different stages of development require different solutions. Never ask an encyclopedia salesman if you need an encyclopedia. He has the kind of one-size-fits-all mentality that will wreck your business.

Thinking Time

- Where are we relying on the story and not the facts?
- Where have we been "sold" (or are currently implementing) a solution for the problem that isn't?
- What solutions are we currently executing that are no longer relevant, given the shift in the environment over the last three to five years? (For a tragic real-world illustration of this mistake, read the chapter "Mann Gulch.")
- Where have we made the fatal mistake of attempting to move away from our problems instead of fixing them?
- Where are we relying on "experts" to sell us solutions instead of first identifying the core problem that needs to be solved?
- Where are we throwing resources at the problem instead of resourcefulness?
- What solution have we created that is not working because we don't have the skill set, experience, or bandwidth to successfully execute?
- What are the obvious problems we are experiencing and what needs to be done about them?
- What opportunities in front of me require additional knowledge or new skills?
- What are those skills and where can I best acquire them?
- Where are the life-threatening problems we are experiencing and what needs to be done to course-correct, fix them, or reduce the risks ASAP?
- Where is our business in pain (or what are the bottlenecks/choke points) and, based on this answer, what needs to be done to alleviate this pain?

- What have we been doing or thinking that we need to stop or change in order to accelerate our growth and profits?

NOW . . . Go Think! You will thank me later.
KJC

CHAPTER 25

YOU, INC.

The financial tooth fairy crowd never seems to tire of encouraging their sheep to abandon their "job" in favor of "owning a business." The conventional wisdom and logic seems to be that you have a job if you sign the back of the paycheck and a business if you sign the front; that if you work for the man you are a failure and a loser. This is intergalactically stupid advice!

Every successful business Owner I know or have read about has a job in the business they own. The job probably does not resemble the job they used to have when the business first started, but they do have work they must do (a job) in addition to being the Owner of the business. In most successful businesses, the Owner runs the business end of the business, but that is a job too. (In the chapter "A CEO Should *Never* Delegate . . ." I explain that particular job in more detail.)

Quitting your job to start a business makes as much sense as buying a bigger bed when you don't like the person you are sleeping with. Unless you have the requisite *business* skills and tools required to be successful as a business Owner, you will forever be frustrated and tired . . . and probably fail.

Webster's defines a job as an activity that gets done for pay. A business is defined as a commercial activity involving the exchange of money for goods or services. They sound remarkably similar, don't you think? That's because they are.

Too many people make the mistake of believing that the key to business success is business ownership and voting control. The truth is, your effectiveness as the CEO of your own business is directly correlated to your effectiveness as an employee of someone else's business. If you party until 2:00 a.m., roll out of bed at noon, are consistently late to work, and haven't read a book or taken a course to improve your skills in the last three years when you have *a job*, you will do the same things if you *own your own business.*

If your level of intensity and work ethic are MIA at your job, things will be no different if you are the "boss." If you spend money you don't have by maxing out your credit cards, have no savings for a rainy day, and never balance your checkbook when you work for someone else, you will drag these same behaviors with you if you are the Owner. (*Hint:* You cannot have financial freedom without financial discipline.) If you do just enough to get by as an employee, you will do just enough to get by when you start your own business.

I know what you're thinking. "Keith, I am not like other people." "Keith, you don't understand my situation." "Keith, if you just knew how horrible my boss is, you wouldn't put in the full amount of effort you are capable of, either."

I have heard all these excuses and justifications from a multitude of whiny people who have tried to convince me that somehow they are the exception to the rule. I'm not buying it.

As my friend Harv Eker likes to say, "How you do anything is how you do everything." He is a smart man.

Consider this: Every rich person I know has a job to do at the company they work for. And every one of these successful people "owns" their job. Sometimes the job they own is for a company they own and sometimes the job they own is for a business controlled by others. Either way, they have taken ownership of their work—the work performed and the outcomes produced. The job, like everything else in their life, is an extension of their identity and the narrative they have created about who they are and how they will perform their work. ("Help Me Understand" is a great chapter to refer to for more ideas on "owning your job.")

Warren Buffett has a job to do. (Warren only owns 33% of his company, but he controls it. Control is about being good at what you do, not the percentage of votes owned.) No one has to beg him to do it. He owns his job and is constantly striving to get better at it. He practices very hard, pays attention to his results, and learns from his mistakes.

So do Michael Dell and Larry Page. They have an office, go to meetings, take telephone calls, manage the organizational structure, approve strategies, hire and fire employees, create budgets, measure execution, communicate with stakeholders, do work, think hard, and get paid for doing it. That's a big job! But it's still a job. (In "Something for Nothing . . . *Seriously?*" you'll find still more on this subject.)

The reality is that different opportunities (jobs) require different skill sets. Great business owners aren't born with business knowledge. The successful ones studied, practiced, and mastered the art and science of business leadership, leverage, planning, and measurement. If you happen to have "business Owner" as one of the jobs you need to perform, you will need to learn the skills of business ownership in addition to the skills of your profession.

I call one of my favorite Thinking Time sessions "YOU, Inc." You (as a person) are the CEO of YOU, Inc. As in all organizations, someone must be actively engaged in managing a host of activities to be successful—things like production, finance, accounting, operations, marketing, sales, advertising, R&D, wellness, quality of relationships, training and development. In your life, you are the CEO of you. You are the only person responsible for all these areas.

Unlike most CEOs of a business, however, you do not have a Board of Directors of You, Inc. that you report to. But, what if you did? What if you had a Board that had followed you around all day, every day, for the last seven days? They had seen every click of your mouse, the level of intensity of your focus, how you planned and prioritized your work. They had seen everything you did as CEO of YOU, Inc.

Ask yourself this question: "If I had a Board of Directors, would they give me a raise or would they fire me?"

Here it is on a bumper sticker: If YOU, Inc. were a publicly held company with stockholders, would your stock price be rising, falling, or treading water?

Thinking Time

- Where has the "job" mentality of comfort zone, path of least resistance, and "do the least expecting the most" crept into my thinking and performance?
- Where are the growth opportunities that I have been postponing because they require extra effort or are outside my comfort zone?
- What business skills do I need to learn so that I can create the leverage required to be a successful Owner? Who can I learn them from?
- How important is learning this business stuff and how fast do I need to learn it?
- Who do I have on my team that is performing at a level of "just enough to get by" instead of really stretching and going for the gold medal?
- How do I define excellence? Why shouldn't that standard be the standard I work toward regardless of my ownership percentage?
- If I had a Board of Directors, where do I need to pick up my game to deserve the raise (incremental profits) I am seeking?

NOW . . . Go Think! You will thank me later.
KJC

CHAPTER 26

KEEPING THE
LUG NUTS TIGHT

Change can happen as a result of an external environmental adjustment (competition, governmental regulations, interest rates, consumer preferences, etc.) or from an internal structural shift.

More often than not, the internal changes we experience are a result of entropy. Without regular attention and maintenance, progress decays, advancement slows, and success erodes. This problem of natural deterioration is compounded by the well-known adage "success breeds complacency."

As soon as we get good at something or achieve a milestone, we take our foot off the gas. We stop doing the things that caused the successful outcome and, as a result, often undo the progress we just made.

Equally damaging is the typical MBA school obsession with finding and fixing problems vs. keeping problems fixed. It is analogous to being the race car driver who obsesses about tight lug nuts on the wheels vs. tight lug nuts on the wheels that stay tight—two different problems that require very different solutions.

You and I have both experienced the frustration of finding and fixing a problem only to have the wheels come off at exactly the wrong time. (Is there ever a good time for the wheels to come off?) If we were being completely honest here, we would acknowledge that the "fix" was not really a fix, only a patch, hence the subsequent wobbly wheels.

Most business gurus will tell you that the key to keeping lug nuts tight is developing a system for tight lug nuts. My forty-five years of business experience suggest that defaulting to a system as the solution for tight lug nuts is dangerously shallow and usually produces debilitating 2nd-order consequences (red tape and bureaucracy). Systems are wonderful for creating consistency but rarely result in excellence. (Take a look at the chapters "Systems vs. Flexibility" and "The Advantage of Being Small" to think about this in greater depth.)

Keeping problems fixed is all about the culture. (The chapter "Culture Is King (You Get What You Tolerate)" will give you lots to think about in creating a culture that keeps things fixed.)

- If you have a culture of training, learning, and improvement, the lug nuts will remain tight.

- If the culture is based on measuring, personal accountability, and ownership of the work being performed, the lug nuts will stay tight. ("The Big 8" details the benefits of having employees create a plan they take ownership of and monitor.)

- If integrity is at the core of an organization's culture, the lug nuts will stay tight. Most organizations think of integrity as ethics or truthfulness. I would like to offer an alternative definition: Integrity is doing what you said you would do or cleaning it up.

The most expensive part of change, whether externally or internally driven, is the inevitable loss of momentum. As one of my mentors told me years ago, "Keith, the problem with always starting over is you are always starting over." The sheer amount of brute force required to get the merry-go-round started again is monumental in comparison to the minimal amount of effort required to keep it greased, maintained, and spinning.

Here it is on a bumper sticker: Keeping the lug nuts tight is a cultural issue, not a systems problem. A culture that loses focus on training, has an unwillingness to measure, and has an aversion to holding people accountable will always result in lost productivity and loose lug nuts.

Thinking Time

- When I look back several years, what has changed (either internally or externally in the environment) that is impacting my results?
- What must I do to confront this issue, fix it, and keep it fixed?
- What are the internal pressures or changes that are impacting my ability to keep the lug nuts tight?
- Where do the lug nuts tend to get loose when we are stressed or near capacity?
- What problems are we repeatedly solving (or are remaining unsolved)?
- Where (exactly) has the culture of training, accountability, and integrity been sabotaged by an obsession with fixing the problems vs. keeping the problems fixed?
- In our quest for size and speed, what are the changes that have caused the foundation to crack and the fundamentals to erode?
- What changes must I make to our culture if these problems are to be fixed once and for all?
- I know there is a big difference between doing and done. What needs to be finished?

NOW . . . Go Think! You will thank me later.
KJC

CHAPTER 27

THE APOLOGY

If the culture in your business is to change, then it will start with you apologizing to your employees.

The lousy culture you have now was created by you. It is a perfect reflection of what you have tolerated and therefore is your fault. The apology is the beginning of the culture change process and communicates your culpability in the toxic environment you currently have as well as your courage and commitment to create a new environment. (See the chapter "Culture Is King (You Get What You Tolerate)" for lots more on this topic.)

What follows is a draft of the apology speech I have given when faced with a need to do a hard restart of the culture in a business.

I owe you an apology. I did not do my job. I have allowed my lack of courage and desire to keep the peace to get in the way of being a leader. I tolerated the status quo and mediocrity because I didn't want to have the hard conversations. I mistakenly believed it was more important to keep the peace than to have the courage required to lead.

I admire and respect you, but I have let my admiration for you cloud my judgment and my willingness to say what needs to be said. Candidly, I have probably functioned in a friend and peer role and not in

*an Owner and leader role. I elevated being liked over being success-
ful. I have been more in love with the tranquility than I have with
our outcomes.*

*One of the transitions all successful businesses must navigate is
from mom-and-pop free-for-all (let's all pitch in and get it done)
to a more professional, disciplined management kind of structure. I
made the mistake of giving people big titles and extensive latitude
in the erroneous belief that this would produce an outcome-driven,
results-oriented organization in which people were accountable for
their results. I was wrong.*

*What I need to do is what every sustainably successful organization
in the history of mankind has done, and that is to transition from
being a company of ideas, fire drills, drama, and fuzziness to a company of outcomes, standards, accountability, and results.*

*The truth of the matter is we can have the best vision and mission state-
ment in the world, but if no one has a clue as to how that translates to*

- *an obstacle we must overcome*
- *an outcome we are striving to achieve*
- *an executable plan*
- *a set of critical driver activities*
- *a standard of excellence*
- *a dashboard that gives us optics*
- *accountability and ownership*

*then we have no shot at accomplishing that mission or delivering on
those values.*

*If no one knows exactly where we are and exactly what we are try-
ing to accomplish, we will not understand the problem we are trying
to solve or the gap we are trying to close. If we don't have clarity of
exactly what the obstacle is we are attempting to overcome, how do
we prioritize resources or build a machine that allows us to get from
here to there?*

If you look at an F-16 fighter jet, the sophistication of the dials and dashboards is breathtaking. Why is that?

Because an F-16 is a high-performance machine. If a mistake is made in an F-16, someone is likely to die. Compare that to a tricycle, a low-performance machine. It has no cockpit or dashboard. It does not go very fast and takes a ton of manual effort to get from here to there. If a mistake is made on a tricycle, the worst that happens is a scab on your knee.

The higher the performance or the faster you want to go, the greater the need for a cockpit of dials and dashboards. The greater the need for precise measurements, standards, structure, and accountability.

Pilots of high-performance machines do not fly by the seat of their pants. Yet I have tolerated a culture of "hand crank" tricycle performance, which helps explain why we are not achieving our full potential for our stakeholders. We have high maintenance and I am optimizing for high performance.

Here is where I need your help. What I want us to do is identify the obstacles that are in our way, design the strategy and build the machine that will allow us to overcome these obstacles, prioritize and thoughtfully allocate the resources required, measure our results against the standards we have set, and hold everyone accountable for their part of the process.

We will have three rules of the game:

1. *Rule #1: Do the right thing.*
   a. *Have a plan, work the plan.*
   b. *Measure your results.*
   c. *Be accountable—see it; own it; solve it; do it.*

2. *Rule #2. Do the best you can.*
   a. *Turn problems into opportunities.*
   b. *Add value by becoming part of the solution.*
   c. *Act with a sense of urgency . . . Do it now!*

    d. Ask the question: "What else can I do?"

    e. Ask for coaching: "What can I do better?"

    f. Reject average and "good enough."

    g. Learn, correct, improve, and grow.

  3. Rule #3: Show others that you care.

    a. Show respect.

    b. Say: "Please. Thank you. You're welcome. I'm sorry."

    c. Show and express appreciation.

    d. Have each other's back ("I got you!").

    e. Engage as a team.

If we do these things and play by these rules we will close the gap. Not only will we close the gap, we will build a high-performance team.

So, here is the question you each need to answer: "Do I want to be a part of helping me create this *team?"*

Deliver this speech to initiate the change and create the culture that will drive the performance of your business.

Thinking Time

- I know that making the decision to give the apology speech is just the beginning. What are the specific follow-on initiatives I need to consistently execute to ensure that the speech sticks?
- What are the rituals I must create to help us reinforce and follow through on this message?
- Where do I need to get clarity about the opportunities we must create to continue the dialog and messaging about the culture we are creating?
- How can I instill the ownership of these rules in my employees so that they become the guardians of our culture?

NOW . . . Go Think! You will thank me later.

KJC

CHAPTER 28

HOW AM I GOING TO PLAY THE SECOND HALF?

Twenty-eight years ago I lost all my money. I mean all of it! There was a huge economic upheaval (similar to what happened in 2007–2008), and I was caught with too much optimism, a ton of debt, and no contingency plan. (See "A Crisis Is a Terrible Thing to Waste" for more on this topic.) In reality I was arrogant, complacent, and just plain stupid. I had used my emotions and glands to make business and investing decisions. I did not question my assumptions and had never considered the possible risks and 2nd-order consequences of many of my choices. Dumb!

I don't know what misfortunes you have had in your life, but this was a very, very rough time to be Keith . . . partially because I suffered a major loss, and partially because my self-worth was entwined with my net worth. A deadly combination!

I have since learned that how you run your business during the good times is a perfect reflection of how well you will survive the bad times. I was foolish and insanely optimistic leading up to the crash. I had been smoking my own exhaust and had generally been a very poor businessman during the good times. As Warren Buffett says, "You never know who is swimming naked until the tide goes out." Well, the tide went out and the emperor had no clothes.

I went into a very, very severe kind of funk (most shrinks would have diagnosed me as clinically depressed bordering on suicidal).

My comeback from this dark place was a result of a critical distinction I learned from a great teacher. The analogy I use to explain this concept is basketball. Imagine being a basketball player and it's halftime. As you are trotting off the court to go to the locker room and prepare to play the second half, you glance back at the scoreboard. It's 87 to 3 . . . and the other guy's winning.

My "halftime" sabbatical lasted for seventeen months. I grew a pony tail, got my ear pierced, started meditating, and immersed myself in the world's religions and great philosophers in my attempt to figure out the answer to this question: "How do I win this game?" I asked myself repeatedly, on a daily basis, "How do I win this game? How do I win this game?"

Ultimately, I realized that this is a stupid question. The question is not, "How do I win this game?" The question is, "How am I going to play the second half?" I am not going to win this game, but I do have an opportunity to decide how I will play it.

I decided to play for keeps. To do whatever I needed to do to achieve the success and fulfillment I wanted in my life. I decided to play at the level of mastery, excellence, commitment, practice, growth, and contribution.

During my sabbatical, this same very wise man told me the most profound thing I have ever heard (I think about this every day): "Hell on earth would be to meet the man you could have been."

I want be able to meet the guy I could have been, look him in the eye, and say, "I know you . . . because I *am* you!"

James Michener (a seriously great author) had an equally insightful thought about this.

The Master in the art of living makes little distinction between his work and his play, his labor and his leisure, his mind and his body, his information and his recreation, his love and his religion. He hardly knows which is which. He simply pursues his vision of excellence at whatever he does, leaving others to decide whether he is working or playing. To him he's always doing both.

The key to mastering the art of living starts with defining your vision of excellence!

Here it is on a bumper sticker: There is a big difference between success and excellence. Success is getting there. Excellence is staying there.

Thinking Time

- What is my vision of excellence?
- Where is my level of engagement and intensity of focus inconsistent with that vision and the outcomes I desire?
- What needs to happen for me to be one of the top ten experts in my field?
- Where am I dabbling (doing just enough to get by) and what needs to be done about it?
- If my vision of excellence is mastery, what needs to change and how would I live my life?
- Where have I focused on success (getting there) and am missing the distinction of excellence (staying there)?

NOW . . . Go Think! You will thank me later.
KJC

CHAPTER 29

EXECUTION

The solution to a problem is really just another word for your "strategy." The strategy is your *idea* about how you will overcome the obstacle that is preventing you from obtaining the desired outcome.

The success of all strategies ultimately depends on execution. You can have the greatest strategy in the world, but if the strategy is not consistently executed, it will fail. The obvious corollary is that a poor strategy perfectly executed will also fail.

My experience is that most people don't have what they want in their lives because they consistently select solutions they either cannot or will not consistently execute. Deciding on a solution that is inconsistent or misaligned with the requisite skills/resources, coupled with erratic execution, fails.

If you consult any MBA textbook or business guru on the subject of strategy, you will be instructed to select a strategy first and *then* figure out what skills, tactics, or resources you need to execute the strategy selected. The experts will tell you that strategy should determine skills, tactics, and resources. Said in plain English, this means the plan should dictate the execution. I think this is a great theory, but unfortunately it is fraught with problems and will work only if you have unlimited time and money.

We have all witnessed great plans and elegant solutions that never materialize because the strategy is not grounded in the reality of commitment, skills, expertise, resources, and available time. (A footnote to this point: Time is the enemy of choices. The shorter the time, the fewer the choices.)

Management teams that consistently fix their problems and achieve their outcomes invariably look first to their existing/accessible skills, capabilities, and resources before deciding on a course of action and a final solution.

Here it is on a bumper sticker: Start where you are. Don't let perfect get in the way of possible. Or as my dad used to tell me, "Shiny shoes don't help you walk any faster." I'll say this a different way: the goal is not to get the anchor all the way back into the boat. To make forward progress, we only need to get it a quarter of an inch off the bottom.

Prior to selecting any solution to a situation in need of improvement, check your assumptions about:

- What am I really capable of doing?
- What am I willing to do?
- Is this solution congruent with our existing (or easily acquired) skills, resources, and level of commitment?

Without this sober evaluation and honest assessment, the tendency will be to put rubber on the sky and not the road . . . a prescription for the status quo. (Check out the "My Biggest Problem" chapter for more on this one.)

Here it is on a bumper sticker: A good idea for you could be a bad idea for me. It depends on our respective ability, resources, and willingness to consistently execute. (Read "The Bathrobe Theory of Business: When a Good Idea Isn't" to further understand this point.)

Thinking Time

- What is the problem I am trying to solve? (Not the symptom. THE problem! Go brush up on Core Discipline of Thinking #2.)
- What is the obstacle or challenge that is preventing me from being where I want to be and achieving what I want to achieve?
- Is the strategy we currently have not working because it is a strategy we are not consistently executing on, or is it a bad strategy?
- How much of my lack of progress is a result of a lack of consistent execution?
- Where have I built a strategy that we simply cannot (or will not) execute?
- What can I do today to improve my situation?
- What are the existing (or easily acquired) resources, strengths, and underutilized assets at my disposal?
- What would I do if I only had $1,000 to spend on a solution? $10,000? $1,000,000?
- Where have I let a lack of resources become the roadblock for my resourcefulness?
- How could I solve this problem by suspending some of the "rules" (as I know them) and fighting a guerrilla war?
- What great "strategies" have I hatched in the past that are viable but are not getting executed?

NOW . . . Go Think! You will thank me later.
KJC

CHAPTER 30

STRATEGIC GROWTH

Here it is on a bumper sticker: You can't create a strategy or prioritize your resources until you have clarity on the opportunity and the obstacles preventing progress toward the attainment of that opportunity (outcome).

The concept of "strategic growth" implies two things:

1. A realistic understanding of where your business is at present (Point A) coupled with a clear outcome or objective which you want to reach (Point B). Understanding Point A *and* Point B gives you clarity about the gap you are dealing with. Clarifying the gap is critical, because residing in this gap is the obstacle that is preventing forward progress from here to there. All obstacles are in the gap between where you are and where you want to be. If you cannot identify a gap, the obstacle isn't even on your radar. (Take a moment to reread Core Discipline #2—Separate the Problem from the Symptom, and Core Discipline #5—Create the Machine, in "The 5 Core Disciplines of Thinking" to help you grasp this point.)

   Here it is on a bumper sticker: A strategy is the *idea* about what needs to happen to overcome the obstacle preventing forward progress. Without clarity about the core problem (the obstacle), a plan (the specific action steps required to implement the strategy) is a waste of time.

Southwest Airlines got rich because of a very simple strategy: A plane on the ground makes no money. This simple strategy is the guardrail that informs all their decisions. Food, assigned seats, first-class, and multiple kinds of aircraft all defeat the primary strategy of keeping planes in the air. As it turns out, the key to making a ton of money in the airline industry revolves around the airline's ability to load and unload passenger baggage efficiently. Who would have guessed that financial success in the airline business is extreme expertise at baggage handling? If you ever see Southwest start to serve food or install a first-class cabin, short the stock. You will get rich!

2. A willingness to realistically think through the existing internal assets and external needs/pain that could define an opportunity for leveraged growth.

The concept of strategic growth is in sharp contrast to:

- **"Brute force" growth**—which Proctor & Gamble and the remainder of the Fortune 500 engage in. They have massive resources: time, money, consultants, and employees.

- **"Hopium" growth**—which counts on getting lucky and finding a few customers who buy, but never really quite understanding which market segment they represent or why those folks are buying. These customers tend to be very transient and are at high risk of being lured away by the competition.

- **"Tactical" growth**—which subscribes to the theory that increasing the size of the funnel, adding two new salespeople, doubling the conversion percentage, rebuilding the website, and initiating a social media campaign (all tactics) are the one-size-fits-all answer to all growth and revenue problems.

- **"Throw it against the wall and maybe something will stick"**

growth—which relies on the erroneous belief that if you just turn on the faucet, hot water will eventually come out.

In today's world, by far the most common marketing and growth techniques used by management teams are the last two.

The internet, social media, and email blasts have made it easy to let a lot of people know about you, regardless of whether or not they have a need to know about you, much less care about what you are selling. This "buy a bigger bullhorn, find a taller mountain, and scream it at the top of your lungs" approach is a poor substitute for a razor-sharp focus on market segments and on discovering the true pain/problem your product or service solves.

Strategic growth relies on a simple formula:

Internal Strengths + External Needs = Opportunity

Internal strengths require you to think, analyze, and question.

External needs force you to ask, probe, and listen.

Opportunity is only available with structure.

Though this formula is not complicated, the execution of these steps to attain meaningful results is VERY intense and difficult, which is why business success is so elusive.

Step One: The formula for strategic growth starts with internal strengths because no one has the time, money, or expertise to solve every problem the market faces. Without a realistic assessment of our internal leveragable assets, I might have the skills to create great software products but end up selling cheeseburgers because I found a pocket of people who were hungry. I probably know nothing about cheeseburgers and restaurants, but here I am because I didn't start my thinking process with what I know and am good at so I ended up where I didn't plan on landing.

Knowing your strengths and assets is key to strategic growth. A thorough review of your underutilized assets and points of leverage is the critical jumping-off point for designing a strategic growth initiative.

Step Two: You must perform a thorough assessment of the marketplace, the external environment, and the competition. It is critical to realize that the market is not one huge mass but rather a collection of small, sometimes tiny groups of people who have a common, but specific, problem (need/pain). Chances are there is a common denominator for penetrating this target market cost-effectively. They probably have a similar definition of success, for instance. (See "The Triangle of Death" for still more on this business essential.)

We are all aware that you can do the right thing at the wrong time; consequently, paying careful attention to the environment is equally critical in the external assessment process.

Knowing the competition—particularly where the gaps are between what your competitors are doing and where their customers are frustrated—is vital to strategic growth. (The chapter "O Baby!" vividly illustrates this point.) Knowing precisely what the competition is good at and why customers are currently buying from them is a must in researching your strategic growth opportunities.

We want to minimize the brain damage of becoming a "me too" business with no meaningful competitive promise and, therefore, an inability to articulate a valid reason for the customer to make the switch from a competitor to you. I will remind you that differentiation is not a promise.

Step Three: Integrating your internal leveragable strengths with the reality of the external needs/pains/gaps in the market defines the opportunity you should consider pursuing. Part of this analysis requires you to think in terms of buyer segments (niche) and the common denominators these segments will possess.

The opportunity will also give you optics about the level of investment required to pursue a given segment. To make any new opportunity financially successful will require a certain organizational structure and leadership as well as specific skill sets and expertise. You will possibly need to augment your team or incur certain risks to turn this possible opportunity into reality.

Clarity on what you are good at (and can leverage) *plus* clarity on the needs of the target customers and the competition that is currently servicing them *equals* clarity about the opportunity to strategically grow your business with minimum wasted motion, resources, and dumb tax.

Of equal value is an acute understanding of where the market is going. In effect, you are running two businesses simultaneously: the one that is providing revenue today and the one that will generate revenue tomorrow. It is highly unlikely they are the same business. The difference will be what happens externally to cause the transition and what you do internally to respond.

Remember: Sustained success requires strategy. And strategy requires

- clarity on the obstacle or problem;
- a plan to overcome the obstacle;
- a structure for the allocation of resources;
- prioritization of time and activities; and
- an analysis of risk.

A footnote on strategic growth: Marketing is about getting people to notice what you do. Execution is about doing something people will notice. Never assume it is all one and none of the other. Strategic growth requires both! (The chapter "Generalizations Kill Clarity" discusses how this idea relates to creating a plan and measuring outcomes.)

Thinking Time
Internal Strengths (Under-leveraged Assets)

- What special or core skills, expertise, knowledge, strengths, and competencies do we have?
- Do we have any special or leveragable relationships or alliances in our customer list or network of contacts and associates that could influence (or give us access to) groups of potential target buyers?

- What are the key alliances, testimonials, or "influencer" relationships we have (or could develop) that would influence potential buyers?
- Competitively, why do customers buy from us? Why isn't this strength sufficient to cause more potential buyers to stop doing business with our competition and to start doing business with us?
- What is the key positioning statement or compelling promise of our brand?
- What is the excess capacity we currently have or excess resources we currently enjoy that are underutilized?

External Needs (Environment-Competition-Pain)

- Different buyers have different outcomes, priorities, and definitions of "success." Since we cannot be strong everywhere, what is the niche I need to focus on that has a problem/pain I can solve?
- What are the primary pains/problems within this market?
- What is this market most afraid of or frustrated about?
- Where is this group of customers frustrated by the gap between what they want and what the competition is delivering?
- What specific problem do they need to have solved?
- What is the primary gain this target market wants to get?
- People buy products to meet a need. What is their motivating need?
- Where is our competition weak or deficient in delivering the outcomes and value ("success proposition") this target market demands?
- Who are the decision makers, and what is the best way to access and communicate with them?
- Are there any unique circumstances or market segments that would require special communication or decision-making considerations?
- Are there any attractive market segments I could penetrate by finding a large group of potential customers that have a common problem and are already in close proximity? (In other words,

under the theory that birds of a feather flock together, if I am selling running socks, can I access the local running club or get an endorsement from the National Joggers Association?)

Opportunity

- Based on our internal leveragable strengths and the external competitive environment, what are the specific ripe market segments we have identified as an ideal target customer?
- How is this target different from our current customer base?
- What are the additional resources (money, manpower, skill sets, marketing, and expertise) we need to acquire to successfully get traction with or penetrate this market segment?
- Does our organizational chart have some holes/upgrades that need to be filled in light of this new strategic opportunity?
- What risks does this new opportunity represent? What could go wrong? How much capital needs to be invested to adequately fund this opportunity? Can I live with the consequences should these risks occur?
- What is the clear positioning statement and compelling promise that must be communicated to the target market segment?
- What are the specific communication channels required to successfully reach the decision makers?
- What are the core activities that must be prioritized to ensure the success of this growth initiative?
- What are the noncore activities that need to be eliminated or deprioritized?
- What are the clear strategic priorities (projects) that must be implemented this quarter?
- What are we optimizing for?
- What are the specific numerical targets this new initiative is projected to achieve?

NOW . . . Go Think! You will thank me later.
KJC

CHAPTER 31

SYSTEMS VS. FLEXIBILITY

Have you heard the advice that says you should systematize your business to the point that you could leave it for months at a time and, when you got back, it would be better than when you left? That's as illogical as it is stupid.

Systems are an amazing tool that worked incredibly well 200 years ago during the Industrial Revolution. Systems are exceptionally useful when the work being performed is repetitive (think assembly lines and flipping hamburgers) and doesn't involve customer interaction, or when the environment is totally stable. But inject a little volatility and human interaction, and systems become your worst nightmare. Systems foster the illusion of "safe" (it has worked so far) and keep you tied to a "this is how we do things around here" mentality (policy manuals). (I discuss related ideas in "The Advantage of Being Small.")

When the environment changes, which it seems to be doing with ever-greater frequency and severity, the old way of doing things is a killer . . . literally. If you are in a business that is not experiencing radical, mind-numbing change, you are in a parallel universe with which I am not familiar.

Systems can be a useful tool when used in the appropriate situations and in the appropriate amount, but systems are *not* the Holy Grail of business success any more than a hammer is the Holy Grail of carpentry.

If systems were the key to success, the federal government of the United States, United Airlines, and Obamacare would be the most revered institutions on the planet. They're not, so the facts don't support the theory. These guys have put systems on steroids and have policies and procedures down to a fine art . . . and look how much fun they are to deal with. They have prioritized rules and systems and thus become a culture of rules, not excellence.

The one trick pony the "something for nothing, instant success" business authors continually trot out to justify this obsession with systems is McDonald's. Their theory goes like this: McDonald's is extremely successful; McDonald's has extreme systems; ergo, if you want extreme business success, systematize your business to such an extent that it virtually runs itself. You could actually leave it for months at a time and things would not be much better or much worse when you got back. This makes as much sense as duplicating the reserved employee parking policy at Amazon with the belief that by doing so you will replicate their success. ("The Bathrobe Theory of Business: When a Good Idea Isn't" points out the foolhardiness of this mindset.)

Here it is on a bumper sticker: Correlation is not causation. God is love. Love is blind. Ray Charles is blind . . . but that doesn't make Ray Charles God.

In other words, systems worked for McDonald's because they are not people-dependent. The parts *are* interchangeable. If one hamburger flipper doesn't work out, no worries; simply slide another guy into his slot, have him read the six-inch-thick employee manual, and everything runs just like before. Just make sure the flipper doesn't "think" or "show initiative" or do something stupid like try a new way of flipping the patty.

What these pseudo business experts would have you believe is that the biggest mistake you could make is to have your business dependent on the person who is performing the task, hence, the desirability of the almighty system.

It makes me wonder why the winners of the Super Bowl or the World Series or the World Cup place so much emphasis on drafting the right person for each position and not relying on a "system" of interchangeable parts to win championships. It also makes me wonder why super success-ful companies (Google, Apple, and Facebook) spend so much time think-ing about, recruiting, hiring, onboarding, and retaining exceptional talent. It might have something to do with Ray Charles not being God.

The truth is, customers do not care about how efficient you are because of your systems or your unbelievably stupid "press 1 for maintenance, press 2 for support" phone system. Nor do they care what your "company pol-icy" is to make sure that everyone gets treated the exact same way (which is always convenient for the business and not so much for the consumer).

Customers want someone who will fix their problem and make them feel special. That's hard to do when the organization is obsessed with their internal systems and rigid compliance with the policy manual. As Dr. Ichak Adizes said in his brilliant book *Managing Corporate Life-cycles*, "The greater the energy expended on internal systems, the less the energy spent on external focus and growth."

Every successful business Owner I have ever met tells me their most important asset is "My people!" And, they are right. A successful busi-ness relies on the creativity, adaptability, commitment, passion, engage-ment, intensity, intellect, and curiosity of its employees.

When systems get overcooked or put on steroids, the result is pain-ful for customers and employees alike and, ultimately, profits. You know this is true because you have experienced it:

- red tape
- not my job
- limited flexibility
- zero passion
- no curiosity or proactive learning
- the intensity of a sloth

Here it is on a bumper sticker: Systems are great at draining an organization of passion and flexibility. Use them carefully or you will pay a very heavy dumb tax. Besides, how can you deliver exceptional service if you are unwilling to make exceptions? Who do you know that doesn't want to be the exception to all the stupid rules and policies we are forced to deal with on a daily basis? I rest my case.

Thinking Time

- Where have I allowed "our process" and way of doing things to become more important than the customer?
- If I honestly assess the attitude of my employees, where have I let the system be more important than their spirit?
- Where have I allowed a reliance on systems and perks to be a substitute for culture?
- Where have I allowed a reliance on systems to be a substitute for learning and education?
- Where do we need to start making exceptions to be exceptional?
- How do we need to change our processes or systems so that we're more customer-centric?
- Where have we allowed an internal focus on systems replace an external focus on our customers' needs and convenience?
- Where could I give my employees an opportunity to grow, learn, and contribute their ideas so they would engage in their work at a deeper level?
- Where could I allow our employees to be self-directed and in greater control of their processes and outcomes?
- Where have we relied on policy manuals to be a substitute for training and trust?
- Where am I letting the need to do it "my way" or the "right way" get in the way of meeting my employees' needs and my customers' expectations?
- Where have we stopped learning and grown calcified because of a system that either needs to be abandoned or seriously tweaked?

NOW . . . Go Think! You will thank me later.
KJC

CHAPTER 32

CORRECTING THE BUSINESS MODEL

When profits are low and cash flow is weak, we typically attempt to turbo-charge our sales by doing the same thing, only louder. While putting your sales and marketing activities on steroids is always exciting, a wise business Owner has many additional levers to amp profits and cash flow.

Sometimes the problem requires a more radical approach: questioning and overhauling the business model. We rarely revisit or reconsider business model issues when thinking about growth and profitability issues, yet the business model is often the saboteur.

A business model asks five questions:

1. How many resources (time-effort-money) have to be invested?

2. Over what period of time?

3. To produce what volume of revenue?

4. Is that revenue adequate to cover the costs of creating and servicing that revenue stream with enough left over to justify the effort and risk?

5. Are the investors (who allocated the resources in #1 above)

provided with a superior return on their investment in the desired time frame?

In other words, the problem could be that you don't have enough customers. Or, maybe you have enough customers, but you aren't charging enough. Or, you are charging enough, but the costs of marketing, servicing, and fulfillment on the revenue are excessive. Or, the costs are in line for this delivery channel, but there are more efficient channels available. Or, the cost of production is excessive, which is screwing up your economics. So many reasons why the model might be broken have nothing to do with amping your sales and marketing tactics.

I suspect you are like me and most other business owners I know who have decided to grow our businesses in an attempt to become more successful. And, like me, you have occasionally experienced less profitability and cash flow as a result of that flurry of activity. Outgrowing your business model is usually visible when your machine starts to rattle or inefficiencies pop up, resulting in smaller bottom line profits and more drama. That's a sure sign you have a business model problem, not a marketing challenge.

Thinking Time

- Why isn't my business more profitable on the amount of sales I am currently producing?
- Where are we incurring costs that do not support either keeping the customers we've got or getting new ones?
- Where is the investment I am making excessive for the returns I am achieving?
- What must happen to reduce the investment and simultaneously increase the returns?
- Is it possible I need to tweak my business model by redesigning the machine?
- Knowing what I now know, if I could start with a blank piece of

paper, what machine would I design and how would I run this business?

- If my Board of Directors fired me and brought in a new CEO, what changes would she make?

NOW . . . Go Think! You will thank me later.
KJC

P.S. Business as usual is NOT a solution!

CHAPTER 33

INDIGESTION (1 + 1 ≠ 2)

Growth is not necessarily more. More is not necessarily better. Better is not necessarily value-added.

Growth is usually a result of finding a new opportunity, which means there will be something new to work on. The new thing absorbs our attention and resources (bandwidth, time, team, and money).

Since resources that used to be allocated to the old thing (tired and boring) are now being funneled to the new thing (fun and exciting), the old thing usually begins to erode and deteriorate because it is no longer receiving the focus and attention that it used to receive.

This problem is particularly acute when the old thing requires a manual hand crank to keep it operating. Hand-crank businesses (low leverage, no machine) consume resources and are difficult to profitably scale.

A requirement of growth is having the engine, machine, and dashboards in place to *maintain* the old thing while the new thing is being created and fertilized. In other words, the lug nuts on the old thing must be tight *and* kept tight if the expectation is for incremental growth. (See "Keeping the Lug Nuts Tight" for more on this subject.)

Let me say it another way: Everything requires maintenance to avoid decomposition and decay. Without the maintenance of the old thing, the net incremental growth, profits, or enhanced enterprise value from adding the new thing rounds to zero. ("Something for Nothing . . . *Seriously?*" dispels the notion of passive growth and success.)

Here it is on a bumper sticker: Most businesses die of indigestion, not starvation. Pouring gasoline into a hand crank does not produce progress; it starts fires.

Thinking Time

- When I look back at the last few years, where have we made the mistake of adding new without simultaneously protecting the old? What lessons do I need to learn?
- Where have I mistakenly assumed that our existing projects are self-sustaining and require little or no ongoing attention?
- What needs to happen to cause our "old" strategies to continue to perform at the current pace with less manual hand crank and adult supervision?
- What assumptions have I made about the continuity of our existing revenue stream if we shift our focus to this new opportunity?
- What processes, people, training, engine, or dashboards do I need to implement to ensure stability of the execution and results of the business while we spin up the new thing?
- Where is our foundation wobbly or unstable in light of the growth we would like to drive?

NOW . . . Go Think! You will thank me later.
KJC

CHAPTER 34

IF YOU WANT TO GROW . . .

When it comes to growth, the single most important question we must figure out the answer to is this: "Why are our ideal target customers (the multitudes who know about us, have heard our message, and need what we've got) NOT buying from us?" The answer allows us to shift our message, tweak our product/service, or adjust "how" we do what we do so that we have an opportunity to turn a prospective buyer's no or maybe into a yes. Or, perhaps the answer is that these people never were our target customers. Either way, it is a win.

The mistake most of us make in the hope of boosting sales is to keep flogging our products to *new* markets using new communication and messaging tactics. Instead, we should find out why the people we are currently flogging aren't buying. Until this core issue can be identified and addressed, we are a scratch looking for an itch.

Potential customers in your target market who are familiar with your business but still have not bought from you are generally rejecting your solution for one of four reasons.

1. **Risk:** Target customers do not buy if they perceive a risk of failure or have a fear that your solution will not work for them. If they doubt that your product or service will work as effectively or

efficiently as the product they are currently buying or that something could go wrong, they will not make the switch.

2. **Friction:** Sometimes potential customers do not buy because the brain damage associated with switching is too great. They look at all the friction costs that would be incurred and resources consumed in the set-up, retraining, installation, adoption, de-installation, breaking old habits, and implementation of new procedures and processes and realize the pain of the change is not worth the gain. Minimizing friction costs is a critical driver for growth.

3. **The Difference That Makes the Difference:** Confused customers rarely buy. If a potential customer does not have a clear understanding of what you can do for them that is meaningful/important and is not available elsewhere, they are unlikely to make the switch.

    Here is the key: The only way you can describe the difference between you and everybody else who wants their business is to have a granular understanding of what your competitors do and how what you do is meaningfully different. You must be able to tell a customer: "This is what we do and here is why *this* is important and unique. Other venders do not do *this*; they do *that*. If you want *that*, you should buy from them. If you want *this*, you should buy from us." (The ominously titled chapter "The Triangle of Death" underscores the risk of failing to communicate this message. You might also take a look at "Simplifying Growth" for additional thoughts on this subject.)

4. **Success Proposition: Here it is on a bumper sticker:** Value created but not delivered is of no value. Value delivered but not perceived is of no value. In other words, it does no good to wink at a pretty girl with the lights out . . . you're the only one who knows what you did. If you want to get noticed, turn the lights on.

    Most of us have heard the marketing experts refer to a *value proposition* or a "*USP*" (unique selling proposition). And we have learned that the key to growth and success is adding more "value" than the other guy. A far more powerful way to think about value propositions and USPs is to reframe them as a *success proposition*. We need to clearly communicate to potential customers that our product or service/experience (what/how) will meet their definition of success. (The "Strategic Growth" chapter offers insights on how to achieve this in your business.)

This also applies to customers who fire us and start buying from the competition. They've been disappointed one too many times by our inability to consistently meet their expectation of success. If we can understand how our current customers and the target customers define success, we will drive more repeat business and win new customers. The growth you want will never be achieved by a slogan of "great customer service." They want *success*, so figure out what that looks like and give it to them! (In the chapter "O Baby!" I describe this concept in greater detail to help you focus on this key issue.)

People say *no* for a reason. Figuring out that reason is a major key to growing the top line. You and your sales team need to continually ask the questions "Why were we not a fit?" and "Why was someone else a better fit?"

Here's a hint: Honing your conversion technique or initiating a social media and SEO strategy is not the same as clarity about:

- what customers (current and potential) want;
- what they are afraid of;
- how they define success;
- how we message the difference that makes the difference; and
- what solution must be designed, promised, and delivered to exceed their expectations and meet their definition of success.

As Peter Drucker insightfully suggested, "The customer rarely buys what the business thinks it is selling."

Here it is on a bumper sticker: Few growth strategies are more powerful than giving the customer *certainty of success.*

Thinking Time
General
- Why aren't my sales 2X bigger than they are today (*really*)?
- Competitively, why do customers buy from us?
- What could happen to cause a potential customer to not buy from me?
- What can I do to eliminate these issues?

Risk
- What is my competition messaging or doing that is causing my ideal target customer to do business with them and not with me?
- What specific risks, concerns, or fears do potential customers perceive that might be blocking their willingness to do business with me?
- If I am asking a customer to stop doing business with someone else and to start doing business with us, what are the risks they are imagining in making this switch?

Friction
- What are the specific friction points that cause customers to hesitate or decline doing business with us?
- How might these friction points be mitigated or addressed?
- What is the frictionless, compelling promise we should make? Is this promise clear, unique, and strong enough to cause them to switch to us?

The Difference That Makes the Difference

- What is the DIFFERENCE that makes the DIFFERENCE to the unsold target buyer?
- Is this difference the difference that makes the difference . . . or is it something else?
- What is the one thing that would be the difference that makes the difference for our target market and cause these people to immediately understand why this difference is important and meaningful?
- Is the message (promise) we are delivering to potential clients clear on the solution we offer that the competition cannot or does not offer?
- How does this message need to be communicated more effectively?

Success Proposition

- How (specifically) does the unsold buyer define "success"?
- Competitively, does the value we are delivering to the client exceed the price we are charging? How do we know? What needs to happen to be sure?
- What expectations do our target customers have?
- How do we meet these expectations more effectively than our competition?
- What must happen to meet/exceed the customers' expectations and cause them to experience certainty of success?

NOW . . . Go Think! You will thank me later.
KJC

CHAPTER 35

ON VS. IN

When is the last time you were introduced to someone and they asked you what business you were "on"? Do you know why that hasn't happened and never will? Because it's a stupid idea!

People don't go around saying, "I'm *on* the technology business." Instead they say, "I'm *in* the technology business." I have never heard anyone say they are *on* a relationship either. People seem to be *in* relationships. The most successful people I know are all *in*.

The psychobabble business literature advocates the toxic idea that if you own an automobile garage and you are the person who is actually changing the oil, aligning the tires, or replacing the spark plugs, you are *in* your business—the insinuation being that *in* your business makes you either inferior or a loser or both.

I have even heard a well-known business consultant say, "You really don't have a business until it can run without you." That is as stupid as it is lethal.

It is true that most small business owners *don't* spend enough time performing the ownership duties of running the business end of their businesses. They *do* spend too much time operating their businesses by doing the actual "oil changes" and, as a result, are tired, struggling, and disappointed.

The problem is NOT that they are *in* their business, however; rather, the problem is that they have not learned the critical *business* skills required to make the shift from "Operator" to "Owner." ("The 4 Hats of Business" and "A CEO Should *Never* Delegate . . ." provide additional insights for how and when to perform these roles.) They haven't learned how to prioritize, allocate resources, hire, delegate, leverage, create a culture, read financial statements, create processes, build the structure, and install dashboards, accountability, and critical drivers. It's not that they don't want to; it's that no one ever taught them how.

Unfortunately, the leap from Operator to Owner is not a smooth one. It is a transition and not an event. It requires a commitment to learning, a bias for being a student, and usually a coach, an advisor, or a mentor. (Trial and error is simply too expensive and takes too long.) *Business* skills are the foundation for *business* success and create value that far outweighs the value created by changing the oil. But they must be learned.

Take a look at the ten wealthiest people on the planet. With the obvious exception of Bill Gates, who decided he needs to figure out a way to make a significant difference on this planet by giving away $100 billion, the other nine are all still *in* their businesses.

I'm not saying that Michael Dell is still assembling computers on the factory room floor or that Phillip Knight is still schlepping tennis shoes out of the trunk of his car. They're not. They are, however, still *in* their businesses. What has changed is their job title, not their level of involvement or commitment. They continue to regularly provide oversight, insight, and wisdom based on their experience. They are "en"gaged and "in"volved, which is what is supposed to happen when you own a business.

The moment you "disengage" from your business, you have shifted from "Owner" to "Investor," and now there needs to be someone else *in* the business to run things.

Regardless of your business, industry, or stage of development, don't ever think for even one minute that your business would be better off without you. If you actually conclude that it would, sell it, shut it down, or hire your replacement, but don't think you can leave it—be *on* it—and make it a success.

Business success has absolutely nothing to do with being *on* and everything to do with determining the most critical success factors and then getting busy learning, prioritizing, allocating resources, and leveraging yourself so that you can successfully run the business end of your business, which is, after all, the job of *every Owner*.

Thinking Time

- If I only had _____, I could spend more time running my business instead of replacing the spark plugs and pumping the gas.
- If I only could _____, I would have more time to run the business end of my business and make more money.
- Where am I confusing activity and sweat with productivity?
- What are the biggest time sucks and choke points that are preventing me from allocating an additional five hours per week to running the business end of my business?
- Knowing the choke points and having the funds to do something about it are two different problems. What are some creative (inexpensive) solutions that would move me in the right direction and alleviate some of the pain?
- What am I currently doing that should/could be outsourced or leveraged to someone else (even part-time) who actually enjoys and is good at the thing that is bogging me down, which would then free me up to do more of the critical, value-add, business Owner activities?
- What critical projects are languishing because I simply don't have the time to allocate to them and get them off the ground?
- What could I do in the next week that would improve this situation?
- How can I prioritize my calendar to find an additional thirty minutes per day to chip away on the high-value projects?

NOW . . . Go Think! You will thank me later.

KJC

CHAPTER 36

NOT ALL RISKS
ARE CREATED EQUAL

Here it is on a bumper sticker: Not all progress is measured by ground gained. Sometimes progress is measured by losses avoided.

The key to avoiding losses is minimizing risk. The prerequisite to minimizing risk is identifying and understanding it in all its forms.

Since risk is about the future, and the future is unknowable, it is impossible to eliminate risk; however, it *is* possible to significantly reduce it.

If you stop to think about the losses you have incurred in the past, more often than not the reasons for these losses boil down to unexamined, excessively optimistic assumptions, inadequate skepticism, and failure to consider what could go wrong. What I'm talking about here is playing defense. It is as true in the business world as it is in the sports world: national champions have a world-class defense. They avoid making bad and erroneously optimistic decisions that cause unnecessary unforced errors.

Losses are the result of one of two things:

Something happening that wasn't supposed to happen.

Something that was predicted to happen didn't happen.

These are called risks. And all risks have three moving parts:

1. The probability of the risk occurring;

2. The cost if it does occur; and

3. The manageability or controllability of the risk identified.

I have created a simple, four-step Risk Assessment tool that I regularly (semiannually) use with all our businesses and when I am making major business or investment decisions. In addition to supporting the creation of enterprise value (I've written an entire chapter—"Creating Enterprise Value"—on this core topic), the Risk Assessment tool helps me think about what could go wrong and how to minimize the cost as well as the likelihood of it going wrong before it happens.

Here it is on a bumper sticker: When you think about what could go wrong, you dramatically increase the odds of creating something that will go right.

RISK ASSESSMENT TOOL

Start by drawing the following chart. Note that you will likely have more than seven lines for your list because more than seven things could go awry.

Step #1 Risk	Step #2 Probability (%)	Step #3 $ Cost (1–10)	Step #4 Controllable (1–10)
1.			
2.			
3.			
4.			
5.			
6.			
7.			

Step #1

Make a complete list of all the risks specific to your situation, business, or investment. Think about all the things that could go wrong. For the purposes of this exercise, it does little good to think about the .01% stuff, like a terrorist attack while you are at the Super Bowl next year—the probability of which is pretty low. But it would make sense to think about someone hacking into your computers with ransomware. Brainstorming, creativity, suspension of beliefs, and brutal honesty are crucial to this exercise.

A great way to do Step #1 is to write a "pre-mortem." You know that a postmortem is an autopsy to determine how the patient died. A pre-mortem is used *before* you make a decision to anticipate problems and their likelihood. You project yourself and your business one year into the future and then mentally look back at the previous year. Imagine that the thing you are about to do has turned into a dumpster fire. By looking back from the future perspective, determine what happened and what went wrong. You are far more likely to be successful if you keep the obstacles and risks in mind when you're designing the solution.

Clarity on the possible risks you face is Step #1 to managing risk.

Step #2

Go back to the top of the list of risks you enumerated in Step #1. Using your best estimate, assign a probability of occurrence next to each risk and record this probability in the column marked Step #2.

The probability of occurrence is expressed in a percentage. For example, if one of the risks you have identified is that interest rates will go up to at least 7% in the next three years, and you think the probability of that happening is 40%, then in column 2, next to that risk, write down "40%."

For this exercise, do not worry about risks that have less than a 2% probability of occurring. These are remote risks. And, while they might occur, we have bigger fish to fry than the bottom 2%.

After you have made an educated, *realistic* guesstimate about the probability of each risk occurring, highlight the Top 10 highest-probability risks (the ones with the highest estimated percentage). The Top 10 will be the ones for you to focus on for the remainder of this Risk Assessment exercise, because they are the ones that are most likely to happen.

Step #3

For each Top 10 risk (only the Top 10), decide if the financial cost of that risk (should it occur) is low [1–3], medium [4–7], or high [8–10]. Then, using your best estimate, assign an estimated cost of occurrence numerical ranking (low, medium, or high) next to each Top 10 risk and record this numerical estimate (1–10) in the column marked Step #3.

A low-cost risk [1–3] is analogous to having a piece of sand in your shoe. It irritates and is not much fun to deal with, but you can still walk and function at 90% capacity.

A medium-cost risk [4–7] is like having a broken leg. Walking is impossible for the short term, but you are still mobile and can function, albeit at a much slower pace and with much greater effort than before you broke your leg. With a medium-cost risk, the incapacitation is for a limited period of time, but the limp is noticeable and changes the way you play the game.

A high-cost risk [8–10] is a total game changer or even death. If this risk occurs, it is a major disruption to the business, a train wreck, or— worst case—bankruptcy. At a bare minimum, a high-cost risk is paralysis that will require years of physical therapy to overcome.

Step #4

For each Top 10 risk (only the Top 10), decide if the risk is controllable [1–3], manageable [4–7], or uncontrollable [8–10]. Using your best realistic guess, assign an estimated manageability of occurrence numerical ranking (low, medium, or high) next to each Top 10 risk and record this numerical estimate (1–10) in the column marked Step #4.

Controllable risks [1–3] are extremely rare because there is very little we can totally control, especially if there is risk attached to it. (I cannot control whether or not I am in an automobile accident, but I can control how fast I'm driving, if I'm wearing a seat belt, or if I'm texting while I drive.)

Manageable risks [4–7] are risks I don't have complete total control over but I can influence or manage the likelihood of them happening or the cost if they do happen. I might not be able to control whether or not my best salesperson decides to leave for another job, but I can certainly influence her decision-making process with the compensation package, title, administrative support, culture, and feelings of importance and contribution to the business.

Uncontrollable risks [8–10] are things like the economy, the price of oil, government regulations, interest rates, and the competition.

Now draw the Risk Assessment bubble chart on the following page.

On the vertical axis you'll plot the financial or monetary cost ranging from high [8–10] at the top of the chart to low [1–3] across the bottom of the chart.

On the horizontal axis you'll plot the degree of controllability, manageability, or uncontrollability of a risk.

Each Top 10 risk will be assigned a circle and be placed on the Risk Assessment bubble chart. The higher the probability that a risk will occur, the larger the circle assigned to that risk.

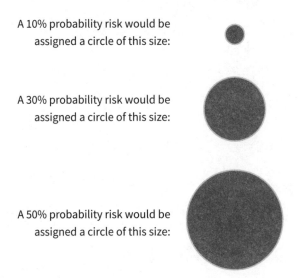

A 10% probability risk would be assigned a circle of this size:

A 30% probability risk would be assigned a circle of this size:

A 50% probability risk would be assigned a circle of this size:

Risk Assessment Bubble

	Controllable (1–3)	Manageable (4–7)	Uncontrollable (8–10)
Cost ($) High (8–10)			
Med (4–7)			
Low (1–3)			

You might have identified risks that have a higher probability than 50%, of course, so your circle size will increase proportionately based on that higher probability.

It'll help if I give you an example. Suppose you identified the following four risks as part of your Top 10 probability assessment:

a. A 75% probability risk that the competition would introduce some product that would cripple your ability to effectively compete. Assume the cost of this was moderately high [7], but because of your branding and ability to innovate, your ability to control the impact is somewhat manageable [7].

b. A 50% probability risk that the regulatory environment would drastically change in the next three years. Assume the cost of this was extremely high [10] and your ability to control this risk is zero [10].

c. A 40% probability risk that the economy would significantly reset in the next two years, thus lowering the demand for your product or service. Assume the cost of this risk is moderate [5] and the risk is completely uncontrollable [10].

d. A 30% probability risk that the key architect of your software code leaves your company for a better opportunity. Assume the cost of this risk, should it occur, is moderately high [6] and the manageability is average [5].

These four examples would be plotted as follows on the next page:

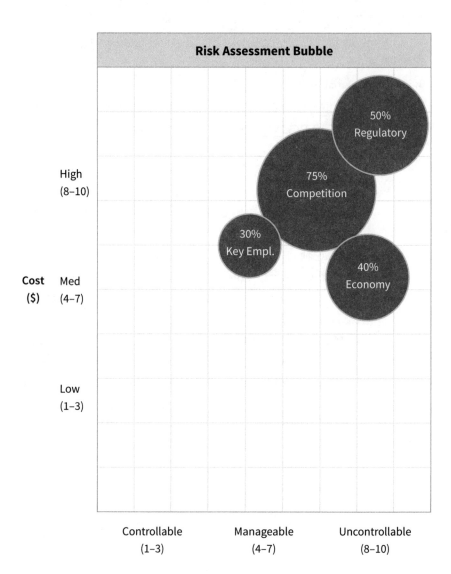

Plotting the Top 10 highest-probability risks on the Risk Assessment bubble chart changes the way you think about and understand the various risks you face.

Identifying and understanding each risk and the three moving parts of each risk—probability, cost, manageability—is a primary job of any leader. Once identified, our job is threefold:

1. Shrink each circle by looking for ways to reduce the probability that each risk occurs.

2. Move each circle down the vertical axis by thinking about ways to mitigate the cost of the risk should it occur.

3. Move each circle toward the left by thinking about ways to control or manage the occurrence of the risk.

Thinking Time is particularly effective in helping you figure out how to reduce the size of each circle and move it down and to the left. I'll say it again: When you think about what might go wrong, you are more likely to design something that goes right.

Taking risks is mandatory for progress. Nothing happens without taking a risk. The goal is not to eliminate risks (although that is always a pleasant fantasy) but rather to identify and understand them by questioning our assumptions, thinking through 2nd-order consequences, planning for problems, and minimizing/mitigating the costs and probability.

The high value from this risk assessment thinking comes in the creation of asymmetrical returns in which the risks of a bad outcome are minimized and the upside return is maximized (thus minimizing the dreaded dumb tax).

Let me leave you with this serious warning: If two or three fairly high-probability risks [7–10] are clustered in the upper right-hand corner of the bubble chart, run! The odds of at least one of them occurring are high enough and the cost severe enough that attempting to proceed is like trying to juggle chainsaws blindfolded; someone is going to get seriously hurt.

Howard Marks (one of the world's most successful investors and the author of *The Most Important Thing*) said it best: "It is more important to ensure survival under negative outcomes than it is to predict maximum returns under favorable ones."

Thinking Time

- If I am truly serious about building a first-class defense and creating sustainable financial success, what are the Top 10 highest-probability risks I am facing right now?
- What is the probability of each risk occurring?
- What is the financial cost of each risk if it does occur?
- How controllable, manageable, or uncontrollable is each risk?
- What can I do to minimize the probability and cost and increase my ability to control or manage the occurrence of each risk?
- Where are we relying on a "dodge all the bullets" mentality to create our success?
- What assumptions have I made about these risks that are wishful thinking and simply untrue?
- How strong is our defense and what can I do to improve our odds?
- Where have we suspended disbelief and ignored skepticism by telling ourselves a story that begins with, "We are different and the rules don't apply to us because . . ."?
- What are the 2nd- and 3rd-order consequences of my current plans and initiatives?
- Where have I let greed and optimism infect our assumptions about the future to the point that I am not identifying or minimizing our risks?

NOW . . . Go Think! You will thank me later.
KJC

CHAPTER 37

THE TRIANGLE OF DEATH

What would your revenue be if you had no competition? How much could you charge? I already know your answers. "Keith, if I had no competition, I could sell everything I could make and charge whatever I wanted!"

Your answers would tell me that the primary determinant of your revenue is how successfully you give customers a reason to discriminate in your favor. Unfortunately, you cannot persuade a potential customer to buy your products/services and not the other guys' unless you can articulate the difference in a clear message: "Buy me and get this. Buy them and get that. If you want this (and I think you do), buy mine."

Business owners tend to be ignorant and dismissive about their competition. They say stupid things like, "Well, no one else is doing exactly what I'm doing." Or, even worse, "I read a book that says we should ignore our competition because they are not our target market." This is really stupid advice, usually given by people who have never done it. Being unaware of what the competition is doing and the message that you need to communicate to create a sale is a big mistake.

The message/promise is what the academics and marketing gurus refer to as a "value proposition," but I am always a little fuzzy about exactly what that means, so I have renamed it a "success" proposition. It seems to me that customers are looking for more than value; they want success. (Study the chapter "If You Want to Grow . . ." and its list of Thinking Time questions to get clarity about this key concept.)

The core of any business strategy is the promise made to the customer of how the business will deliver a unique mix of products, services, and customer experiences. Here is the key thought: The customer has the *only* vote on whether or not that promise was delivered.

A great success proposition describes how your business will attract, retain, and deepen the relationship with your core group of target customers. The power of designing your success proposition is that it will not only communicate to the target market your promise but also dictate the *internal* priorities and skill sets you must master to deliver that promise. (Walmart's promise and priorities are very different from Apple's.)

There are three primary success propositions:

Operational Excellence (Home Depot, Walmart, McDonald's) The internal focus is on costs, speed, and/or quantity of selection. *Hint:* It's hard to be the low-cost provider if you are not the low-cost producer! (Or, as one of my mentors told me forty years ago, "Price is only important when quality is an insufficient substitute.")

Customer Intimacy (IBM, Nordstrom, the neighborhood drugstore) The internal focus is on both the *quality* of the relationship with the customer and *exceptional* customer experience (service).

Product Leadership (Intel, Apple, Tesla) The internal focus is on innovation, functionality, features, and the overall design and performance of the product.

The mistake small business owners make is attempting to be all things to all people . . . a truly bad idea!

My friends in the software development world have a variation on this theme that I call the Triangle of Death. For any software development project, there are three moving parts: time, price (cost), and quality.

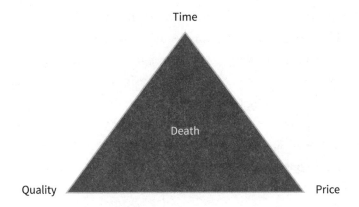

Software engineers will tell you to pick two. For example, a project can optimize for time (speed) and price (cost), but it will have to sacrifice quality (McDonald's strategy).

You would think for a long time to come up with the name of a successful business that has created a great brand by optimizing for all three with equal emphasis. Spectacularly successful companies attempt to excel at only one of these success propositions, maintain parity at a second, and usually ignore the third.

In other words, it is rare (if not impossible) to find a business that delivers the highest quality, in the shortest period of time, at the lowest price, and has a world-class customer experience process. The reason is because that is not a formula for scaling a business or for being profitable. That is a formula for trying to please everyone and, as a result, going broke.

You can make money with any of the three success propositions, but you must prioritize one and then organize the business to master the skill set and internal processes required to deliver on your promise.

Here it is on a bumper sticker: You can't be important everywhere, so be important where it counts.

Thinking Time

- Who is our target market? (This question can never be addressed too frequently.)
- What is our promise to them?

- How is our promise differentiated from our competition?
- How do I know this promise is being successfully delivered?
- Why isn't this differentiation (strength) sufficient to cause more potential customers to stop doing business with our competition and to start doing business with us?
- Where have we let our focus drift from the core (primary) competitive advantage that we have?
- Is this core difference between the competition and us significant enough to cause potential customers to start using us? If not, what is?
- Where have we done a poor job of giving the customer the ammunition to justify using us instead of our competition?
- Where is our messaging weak, ineffective, or simply nonexistent about our core strength (the difference that makes the difference)?
- How does my target customer define success?
- Where are our internal priorities and operational focus misaligned with the promise we have made to our customers?
- Which internal priorities do we need to strengthen to be able to successfully deliver on our promise to customers?
- Where are we internally prioritizing (optimizing) for something we have not promised?
- Where do our team, dashboards, critical drivers, compensation structure, training, hiring, and culture need work so that we are more successful on the execution of the internal processes required to deliver on the success proposition we have promised?

NOW . . . Go Think! You will thank me later.
KJC

P.S. Nobody said this was easy.

CHAPTER 38

MOMMAS LOVE THEIR BABIES

No mother has ever seen her child for the first time and said, "Oh my God! This baby is ugly!" Mommas love their babies. Having said this, I have had mothers show me a picture of their baby, and I can tell you there are lots of ugly babies, just not hers.

Entrepreneurs are the mothers of their ideas and products. They tend to love their idea and become obsessed with the product. Inevitably the entrepreneur will speak about this new project or idea in terms of being "my passion."

This creates two related problems. First, the market does not care how much you love your idea or how passionate you are about it. Your customers do not spend money on your product just because it happens to be your life's purpose. Customers want to get out of pain, avoid a pain, or create a gain, and either you can do that "better" or more efficiently than the competition or you can't.

Second, obsessing about your product or your passion is an internal focus. Optimizing for passion and product perfection instead of customer needs and demand is a classic business mistake. If your intention is to generate sales and make money with your product, then an obsession with the customer is mandatory. Think about it this way: You and your customers are in a relationship. Relationships tend to work best when the focus is on meeting the needs of the other party, not our own.

An interesting corollary is that we are also in a relationship with our business, so the obvious question is: What does my business need to be successful? Does it need structure, better teammates, less drama, fewer expenses, more cash in the bank, less accounts receivable? One of my favorite questions to ask is this: "If my business could talk, what would it say?"

The last time you spent money on something, anything, it was to solve a problem or to meet a need. The business that got your money was the winner based on the *aspirin* they sold and not their *passion* for making aspirin. (You'll want to check out "The 4 Hats of Business" and "O Baby" chapters for more distinctions about this subject.)

Here is the truly bizarre part: You can have a crappy product and still become *über* successful. It's not about the product!

Think of your favorite restaurant. If you were making reservations to celebrate a big anniversary, a graduation, or closing a big deal, where would you eat?

No one over the age of twelve would choose McDonald's. Yet no one has made more money in the history of mankind in the restaurant business than this fast-food giant.

Hearing that statistic you would logically think the reason McDonald's has made all this money is because they have a really good product, right? So let's look at their products. Any of us could make (and have) a better hamburger than McDonald's. (Their French fries are fantastic.) Not only are their cheeseburgers disgusting; if you eat enough of them, it will kill you.

So, here you have the most successful restaurant in the history of mankind, and their product sucks. Not only that, if their customers eat enough of the product, they will have no customers, because they would all be dead. It's not about the product!

I'm not a technology person at all. I came to the technology game late and don't really understand all the digital stuff. The guy who introduced me to computers was a Windows expert, so that's what I use. (I have tried to make the switch to Apple to be cool like my friends, but the friction of learning a new system is beyond my pain threshold.)

All my geeky friends tell me that Apple's operating system is superior to Microsoft's operating system. I have no idea if Apple's operating system is better or not, but my friends and most smart technology experts tell me it is. So, it would be logical to assume that the company with the best product (which also happened to get to the marketplace first) would dominate the market today, right?

Wrong! Turns out, the guy who has the best operating system and got to the market first (Apple) is getting his butt kicked by the guy who got there second with an inferior product (Microsoft). How did that happen? It's not about the product!

Southwest Airlines has made more money in the last twenty years than the rest of the airline industry cumulatively since Orville and Wilbur Wright first flew at Kitty Hawk, North Carolina, in 1903.

It must be because their food is so delicious, their seats are so roomy, the first-class section of the plane is so snappy, and their planes are so state-of-the-art and luxurious, right?

Wrong! Southwest serves no food, and their seats are incredibly uncomfortable: you can barely lean back in them and they're jammed as close together as is humanly possible. They have no first-class or assigned seating, and the planes are the same age as those of any other airline. Yet, they are the only guys in the airline industry that are consistently making money. How are they doing that? It's not about the product!

Name me any product or service; I don't care what it is. Give me a week and I will name one person who has made millions and at least a hundred people who went broke with the same exact idea.

You can probably think of several really good restaurants that have gone broke. You are not seeing any McDonald's going broke. Those guys just keep serving billions and billions and billions. You are not seeing Microsoft go broke. They just keep cranking out code and fixes (they call them updates.)

Could McDonald's, Microsoft, and Southwest Airlines fix their products? Make them tastier, better, or snappier? Of course they could, but that obsession with the product would be unlikely to drive revenue or profits. Here's the truth: They don't have to. They can get filthy, stinking rich with a lousy product.

Here it is on a bumper sticker: Your success will have very little to do with *what* you do and everything to do with *how* you do it. Never, ever forget that.

It's why an inventor's royalty or license fees from a patent are rarely worth more than a token 1–5% of revenue. Ideas are a dime a dozen, but the ability to know *how* to execute on that idea, *how* to differentiate it from the competition, *how* to deliver it, and *how* to monetize that idea is worth 98% of revenue. (Take a minute to reread the chapter "The Big 8" to refresh your memory about this reality.)

We obsess about our passion for our product and the coolness of what we have created instead of doing the heavy lifting to find the pent-up demand, massive frustrations, or serious points of pain in the market and then build a product that meets these needs.

As Peter Drucker says in this regard: "If the marketing is done right, selling becomes unnecessary." (I love this insight so much I cited it in the "O Baby!" chapter too.) He defined marketing as figuring out the red-hot, searing pain and offering a product or service that solves that problem. Aspirin sells itself.

Here it is on another bumper sticker: Instead of falling in love with our products, we would all be more successful if we fell in love with our customers and their outcomes!

Besides, why in the world would I want to fall in love with something that doesn't love me back?

Thinking Time

- Where have we let an obsession with our passion get in the way of an outward focus of finding the group of customers who have a problem I can solve?
- Why are customers buying this product or service and what is really most important to them?

- Where is the red-hot, searing pain or frustration in the market, and what are we doing to address that problem?
- What needs to happen to cause our target market to discriminate in our favor (really!)?
- When I really look at *how* my competition is doing what it is doing to capture market share, what do we need to change to compete more effectively?
- Where do we need to carve out a niche or control some real estate in consumers' minds about our message, our promise, and our results?

NOW . . . Go Think! You will thank me later.
KJC

CHAPTER 39

PRIORITIZING GROWTH STRATEGIES

Different problems in different environments require different strategies. Ask a website expert if you need a new website and 99.9% of the time the answer is yes, regardless of whether or not your existing website is adequate or even relevant to driving your business's growth. Ask a social media guru for advice about growing your business and you will be retaining a social media consulting firm within a week. Guaranteed.

A small group of friends and I were having dinner a couple of years ago with a member of the Forbes 400. During the conversation something came up about nutrition and eating healthy. The rich guy asked the table, "Do you know the biggest problem with having a personal chef?" An innocent question, but it struck all of us as funny because it told us a lot about his world vs. ours. I said, "No, tell me the problem." He replied, "You only get to eat what the chef knows how to cook." The same thing is true for business advice.

The reality is that you can drive revenue any number of ways, depending on what your problem is. Some ways are harder than others, but here's the bottom line: It makes no sense to try to get more when you are not optimizing what you've already got. I'll repeat that: It. Makes. No. Sense.

When it comes to growing revenue, there are eight primary ways (the Growth Funnel chain itemized below) to immediately impact the top line. You should carefully think about how to mix and match these levers to yield the most dramatic results.

GROWTH FUNNEL

1. **Keep More Customers**
(Fall in Love)
FOWTW . . . GAGI . . . GITT

2. **Increase Referrals & Repeats**
("How would you run your business if 100% of your future growth was by referral only?")

3. **Define & Enhance Certainty of Success**

4. **Enhance / Train Sales Process**

5. **Increase Conversion %**

6. **Increase Transaction Size**
(Bonus / Package / Price)

7. **Increase Frequency of Purchase**

8. **Increase Leads / Drive Traffic**

1. **Keep More Customers:** Business owners are notorious for falling in love with their products and the genius of their ideas. The *product* does not have the money, though. The product does not care who owns it. The *customer* has the money. The customer has a specific problem and unmet needs that she wants addressed. She is searching for a solution and someone to do business with that will meet or even exceed her expectations. The primary key to growth is to fall in love with the customer, not the product. (See "Mommas Love Their Babies" if you need more convincing.)

   The most common reason businesses fail to grow is *not* that they aren't adding enough new customers; it's that they aren't keeping the customers they've got.

   Don't believe me? Ask yourself this question: "How big would my business be if I still had every customer who ever tried me?"

   If your growth initiatives are exclusively focused on how to get new customers to try you, you are not focused on meeting and exceeding your current customers' needs and expectations. Adding a new customer is great if you simultaneously keep all your existing customers. But adding a new customer and losing an existing customer is a strategy for treading water and getting tired.

   Keeping customers can be boiled down to three things:

   a. **FOWTW—Find Out What They Want.** Customers do not really care about what you want to sell them, nor do they care how much you love your product. Customers care about having their needs met. The customer gets to define success. We make a mistake when we assume that the genius of our product and our "passion" for our idea are THE most important things. The genius of a great business is a maniacal focus on the customer and his outcomes, frustrations, and success. Steve Jobs said it best: "One of the things I've always found is that you've got to start with the customer experience and work backwards to the technology. You can't start with the technology and try to figure out where you're going to try to sell it."

b. **GAGI—Go and Get It.** After you are clear about the pain, frustration, needs, and expectations of your customers, your job as a business Owner is to find the pain reliever (solution) that meets their outcomes and definition of success. This means designing a solution that specifically addresses your target market's problem in a way that is meaningfully different from what is currently available.

c. **GITT—Give It to Them.** It does no good to find out what customers want, to go and get it, and then not to deliver it to them. GITT is really about the "how" you do it, not the "what" you do. You can give someone a great tasting meal, but an inattentive waiter (or an overly attentive one who interrupts your conversations) will spoil the evening. Alternatively, you can receive an average meal, but the service, atmosphere, and ambiance are so outstanding, the evening is a stupendous success.

(In the "O Baby!" chapter you'll find more customer-centric Thinking Time questions to reflect on.)

2. **Increase Referrals and Repeats:** Here's a question for you: Name me one business that could survive a year without any referrals or repeat business. It's hard to do. I have found that most business owners get so excited about adding new customers they fail to appreciate and show the love to their existing ones. Why offer discounts only to people who have never tried you before? The customers that have been paying our bills for the last ten years are the ones we should be bending over backwards to take care of.

Here it is on a bumper sticker: Sustainable growth requires two things: keeping the customers you've got, and adding new ones.

A great growth question that will help you get clarity on this idea is this: "How would you run your business if 100% of your future growth was by referral and repeat business only?"

Before you decide to start a "Let's grow by adding new customers" initiative, keep in mind it does no good to add them and not keep them coming back. You want raving fans and addicts as customers, which simply means they love doing business with you (because you are successfully meeting their definition of success) and will tell others about their experience.

3. **Define and Enhance Certainty of Success:** The clichés "add more value" and "value proposition" are incredibly overused by marketing experts to describe what your business should deliver to your customers and, thereby, differentiate yourself from your competition. I think about this concept a different way . . . a "success proposition." What has to happen to give your customers *certainty of success*? (I elaborate on the notion of success propositions in "If You Want to Grow . . ." as well.)

   Your customers get to define success, not you. They don't really care about what you want to sell them or how excited you are about your product. At the end of the transaction, they just want to be able to say, "Yes!!! That's exactly what I wanted and I loved it . . . I'll be back!"

   The fundamental success proposition question you should design your business around, especially if you are interested in growth, is: "What has to happen so the customer will say 'I'd have to be crazy to do business with someone else!'?"

   Answering this question will grow your business exponentially!

4. **Enhance/Train the Sales Process:** Most amateurs in business, especially in sales, attempt to "wing it" when it comes to the sales process and presentation. This is a truly bad idea because you will always produce inconsistent results and have no clue what is causing them.

   The best people in the world at sales and sales training have a formula, a script, a process, or a recipe they use. They rehearse and practice that process . . . repeatedly. They rehearse simulated sales processes, ask the toughest questions, raise the worst objections, and then design answers and responses to all of them.

Here it is on a bumper sticker: Mastery = Practicing the right thing in an effort to get better. When the training stops, so does the progress. Candidly, I have found that I am not talented or smart enough to be unprepared.

Attempting to get more leads before training or retraining on the sales process is likely to result in wasted money and burnt leads.

5. **Increase Conversion Percentage:** Obviously, if you get the same number of leads but do a better, more consistent job of closing them, your sales will increase. We know we want to increase the number of customers we have. The low-hanging fruit solution is to increase the closing percentage. If you are currently closing 25% of your leads, a 5% increase in your close ratio is the equivalent of increasing your leads by 20%. (Increasing your conversion or closing ratio is dependent on the training idea outlined immediately above in #4.)

6. **Increase Transaction Size:** Sometimes we have multiple products or services that can be packaged together. When the price of the package is less than the total of the à la carte prices, customers perceive a deal and tend to buy the bigger (higher-priced) package. This is the McDonald's theme of "Do you want fries with that?"

Perhaps you can offer a high-margin, low-cost "bonus" of an ancillary product or service, which would enable you to increase your overall price to the customer but incur relatively minor increases in your expenses.

Here it is on a bumper sticker: Increasing revenue and sabotaging profits is a formula for poor.

The central idea is to design a package that will, for example, increase revenue by 10% and increase profits by 15%. Sometimes the transaction value can be increased with something as simple as a modest price increase. If you have a 10% profit margin, a 2% price increase will have the same bottom line impact on profits as a 20% increase in revenue.

7. **Increase Frequency:** Many successful businesses increase the frequency of customer purchase by helping the customer see the value of shopping exclusively with them. A rewards or frequent buyer program is often used for this purpose. Southwest Airlines does not expect you to fly more frequently as a result of their frequent flyer program, but they are incentivizing you to fly with *them* when you book those next tickets. Loyalty is very powerful because it drives repeat business. Repeat business does not have the usual customer acquisition costs and, therefore, is much more profitable.

8. **Increase Leads/Drive Traffic:** You will immediately notice that this link in the Growth Funnel chain is last on the list. The reason is because it is usually the highest-hanging fruit and consequently the most difficult to attain. In most circumstances, the first seven strategies to impact the top line should be executed and optimized prior to allocating resources to drive the number of leads. **Here it is on a bumper sticker:** Optimize before you maximize.

No one likes to hear this message, because designing websites, writing advertising copy, devising PR campaigns, and creating social media strategies are way more fun and exciting than working on sales scripts, referrals, and repeat business.

When the time is right to work on increasing leads and driving traffic, it is critical to optimize for quality, not quantity. We do not need more eyeballs or visitors to our website; we need to reach our target market with a compelling message.

Here it is on a bumper sticker: Getting big is the result of success. Success is not the result of getting big. One of your jobs is to carefully consider the various strategies available to you for growing your business. Lurching for the "more leads" lever is rarely the best or most effective alternative.

A word of caution: Developing a strategy to grow revenue is important, but growing revenue without growing profits and cash flow is dumb. Successful businesses have figured out how to do both. ("Correcting the Business Model" describes the nuts and bolts of this process.)

Thinking Time
Keep More Customers

- Why do people buy from me in the first place? What value do they seek? Expect? Hope for?
- What is their TRUE pain/problem/frustration?
- What is the compelling promise of our brand?
- Is the message (promise) I am delivering to customers clear on what we can do for them that the competition cannot or does not do?
- What must happen to cause a customer to buy from me?
- What must happen to keep a customer coming back?
- Does the value we are delivering to the client exceed the price we are charging? How do we know?
- What changes do I need to make to my business to ensure my continued relevance to my customers?

Increase Referrals and Repeats

- What percentage of our business comes from repeat customers? Is that percentage growing? By how much?
- What are we doing to ensure that customers will come back for seconds?
- What could we do (that we are not currently doing) to cause our customers to want a second helping of what we are serving?
- How can we get them to come back more frequently?
- How would I run my business if 100% of my future growth was by referral and repeat customers only?
- What promise do we make to our customers?

- Where do we need to realign our internal operations to consistently deliver on this promise?
- What can I do to delight and amaze my customers?
- What can I do to cause my customers to become addicted to buying from me?

Define and Enhance Certainty of Success

- What is my "success proposition"?
- What does my ideal customer consider "success"?
- What are we doing to give our customers "certainty of success"? What else do we need to do?
- What are we doing to meet their expectations?
- What expectations do my customers have that we are not meeting?
- What expectations have I set for my customers, and how are these different from the expectations I am delivering?
- What can I do to cause my customers to say "I would have to be crazy to do business with someone else"?
- Where have we compromised on the trade-offs necessary for my business to deliver on our success proposition?
- Where have we compromised or homogenized our niche by blurring our uniqueness in an attempt to grow?
- What are the activities we perform that are not aligned with each other? Where are we producing a result that is inconsistent with our message?
- What needs to happen for all my employees to know exactly what our success proposition is?
- What are the specific activities each person must consistently perform to deliver this success proposition?
- Where does my dashboard need to be rebuilt to make sure I am measuring and monitoring this performance?
- Where does my compensation structure need to be adjusted to reward performance that delivers on our success proposition?

Enhance/Train the Sales Process

- What is our existing script and process to enroll new customers?
- What is our current internal sales training process?
- What does a first-class training process look like?
- What is the curriculum we need to teach and train in order for our staff to be more effective at initiating and closing a sale?
- What books, videos, manuals, and audio training does our sales team have in their library, and how are these resources getting reviewed and mastered?
- How can we create a "best practices" process in which our team shares the best ideas and methodologies we discover?

Increase Conversion Percentage

- What is our current conversion percentage, what is the target conversion percentage, and what must happen to close this gap?
- What training process do we need to create to increase the likelihood that prospective customers start doing business with us? (Also see the many questions in "If You Want to Grow . . ." on risk, friction, the difference that makes the difference, and certainty of success.)

Increase Transaction Value

- If the formula Value = Benefits ÷ Price is true, what must I do to dramatically increase a customer's perception of value?
- What high-margin product can be bundled with our current product offering that would increase the retail price to the customer and yield an asymmetrical profit margin increase?
- Is it possible to increase my retail price by 2 to 5% and retain our current customer base? (Coca-Cola sells 2 billion units per day. A 1-penny increase in price yields an incremental $20 million/day bottom line profit. Not too shabby!)

- How have we educated our customers about the value of what we do? What needs to happen differently?

Increase Frequency

- What might a loyalty or rewards program for our frequent buyers look like that would cause us to become our customers' preferred vendor?
- What is our niche/specialization/area of excellence, and how can we more effectively communicate this distinction?

Increase Leads/Drive Traffic

- Who is my target market?
- Who can I create an alliance with that also touches or influences this target?
- Where can we find pockets of target customers who are frustrated with our competition? What are we doing to communicate to them that we are the solution they are looking for?
- What is my competition doing that is causing my ideal target customer to do business with them and not with me?
- What is my compelling message to this audience?
- What is the promise of our brand and what must happen to consistently deliver on this promise?
- What do I do for customers that no one else does?
- What can I do for customers that no one else does?
- What should we do for customers that no one else does?
- Do my ideal customers REALLY care about these differences?
- What is my reputation? What am I known for? What is my claim to fame?
- How do customers think and talk about my business?
- How would I like for them to talk about my business?
- What must change for them to talk about me that way?
- What must they be convinced of to start buying from me?

- Why aren't my ideal customers using me now?
- What is the message I need to communicate to cause my target customers to engage with us?
- What are the best communication channels available to communicate this message?

NOW . . . Go Think! You will thank me later.

KJC

CHAPTER 40

CREATING ENTERPRISE VALUE

Business owners and management teams seem to obsess about exiting and exit value, as if exiting was the Holy Grail. The reason so many businesses fail and many of the remainder struggle to find a buyer or are sold for a far lower price than expected (the average small business sells for less than 3.5 times trailing annual "earnings"), is not for a lack of an exit strategy. They all had an exit strategy; unfortunately, they did not have an "exitable business" strategy.

No question, a smart Owner must think long term. But the thinking should be oriented to creating a *sustainable business that minimizes risks*. Do that, and the business is exitable.

Here it is on a bumper sticker: A business that is exitable at the highest possible value has an Owner who is obsessed about the predictability and sustainability of the future stream of earnings.

The greater the predictability and sustainability, the greater the enterprise value and, thus, the more attractive it is to a buyer. Of course, a business with high predictability and sustainability is also a business you might choose to keep (and milk the earnings) instead of exiting, but at least you would have the choice.

The biggest problem with an exit is that, after the sale, you have a ton of cash and no cash flow. So, now you must invest this cash someplace (usually someplace you know very little about) to receive a return, and few returns can match the cash flow of the business you just sold.

Picture this. Suppose your business produced $1,000,000/year of earnings. And assume businesses in your industry are typically valued at four times the earnings because the industry has a higher-than-average predictability and sustainability of future earnings. And imagine that your specific business was unusually attractive and, therefore, commanded a premium multiple of five times earnings. You sell the business, receive $5.0 million cash (assuming your buyer is a cash buyer—an extremely unlikely assumption when dealing with smaller businesses), and now you pay taxes of 20%. Let's assume the taxes are $1.0 million. You now have a remaining balance of $4.0 million that needs to be invested and somehow receive a $1,000,000 annual return (that's a 25% annual rate of return) to match what you were making before.

I don't know about you, but those kinds of returns are not falling in my lap every day, which is why selling a business is tricky. Furthermore, to even come close to that kind of return, I would have to take some outrageous risks (which really means my odds of losing my money just went up).

Candidly, this seller would be much better off financially if she reallocated $100,000 of her earnings to hire her replacement CEO and kept the business for the next ten or fifteen years . . . and then sold it. She could have her cake and eat it too. (Why else would you want cake?)

Regardless of the decision to sell or not, the path to maximizing the enterprise value and creating exitability remains the same: Grow the earnings and control risks.

All businesses have risks, which is simply another way of saying something could go wrong. ("Not All Risks Are Created Equal" offers a great risk assessment tool, and " If You Want to Grow . . ." offers lots more juice on the dangers of risk.)

Here it is on a bumper sticker: The things that *can* go wrong are the things that jeopardize the enterprise value and exitability.

Some risks are identifiable by studying a business's financial statements, which is what my CFO Scoreboard® (available at http://www .CFOScoreboard.com) is designed to do. Some risks are embedded in the structure or framework of the business and are hard to identify by looking only at the numbers. Other risks are environmental (e.g., the economy) and are, by their very nature, uncontrollable, but that doesn't necessarily mean they are unmanageable.

The following is a description of the six critical "non–financial statement" risks an Owner and his management team must address (and continue to monitor) to increase the predictability and sustainability of the future stream of earnings and thus maximize the enterprise value and exitability of the business.

1. **Concentration Risk:** A business that produces $50,000,000 of profits is not necessarily a healthy or even an exitable business. If it has 10,000 customers and one of those customers accounts for 75% of its revenue and profits, this business is in serious jeopardy of failing.

   This is called *concentration risk,* and it happens when the business is too reliant on any one customer, supplier, distribution channel, account receivable, referral source, strategic partner, IT, employee, or Owner. Another way of describing concentration risk is single-point-of-failure risk, meaning that if only one thing goes wrong, Humpty Dumpty can hit the concrete.

   Many founders of a business are comfortable with this kind of risk (until it occurs) because they know the players or companies involved and usually have years of experience living with this risk and nothing going wrong . . . *yet.* Typically, these risks are tolerated on the basis of wishful thinking and misguided assumptions, neither of which are particularly useful when optimizing for maximum enterprise value or exitability.

   What owners of these kinds of businesses fail to appreciate is how these types of risks expose the business to instant extinction in the event of an occurrence. Excessive concentration risk, in any form, destroys exitability and exit values.

   Buyers are uncomfortable with concentration risks and therefore ratchet the purchase price down or simply pass on buying your business. For the majority of small businesses, the Owner is the most significant single-point-of-failure risk, which explains their low exit valuations and difficulty in selling.

2. **Sustainability Risks:** Buyers of businesses are buying the future stream of earnings. Any risk that could disrupt those future earnings impacts the sustainability of the business and therefore minimizes the enterprise value. The greater the risk (or the greater the number of risks), the less the value.

What could disrupt the future stream of earnings? This question goes to the heart of risk analysis and is an extremely important question for all owners to think about. Earnings are a result of revenues minus expenses, so the question I am really asking is: "What could cause revenues to tumble or expenses to soar?" This is a simple question, but it requires serious thought and candor. A business that lacks a clear, sustainable path to profitability is a business that is difficult to exit at any price. *Hint:* Do not confuse sustainability with stability. Volatility is not synonymous with risk.

3. **Business Model Risks:** A business model is the structure of how a business makes money and reveals whether or not the amount made is adequate to compensate the investors for the risks they take. Embedded within this definition are lots of unseen but vital assumptions about the target market, pricing, competition, quality of products, distribution channels, performance guarantees, asset acquisitions, resource allocation, staffing requirements, capital structure . . . and the list goes on.

All business models are subject to both internal and external pressures, which will require you to bend and sometimes break your own model to remain competitive and relevant in the marketplace. You and I both know of businesses that relied on a page-one Google ranking for their primary marketing. The instant Google changed its algorithms, the ranking and the customers vaporized. Google can be risky, too.

Understanding the threats to and weaknesses of your business model is imperative to creating a sustainable and exitable business.

4. **External Risks:** All businesses operate in an environment and are therefore subject to external risks. Something can always go wrong, and often these bad things are not only external to the business but also things we have zero control over. External risks might include your competition, a hatchet job by the crew of *60 Minutes*, a regulatory change, China's GDP slowing down, interest rates skyrocketing, or a repeat of the 2008 economic meltdown.

   Some of these risks might be manageable, but most are probably uncontrollable. Whether the risk is internal or external, manageable or uncontrollable, it is vital that you identify these risks early on and keep your eye on them. Regardless of your firefighting expertise, knowing where the gasoline is stored prior to the fire is critical to preventing the building from exploding in the event of an ill-conceived match.

5. **Leverage Risk:** Adding debt to any financial structure adds risk. When businesses borrow money, the underlying emotion is optimism. More often than not, the money is originally borrowed to facilitate some growth opportunity the management team has identified. And, rather than give up equity, and thereby spread the risk (and the upside if it works), we get greedy.

   The belief is that this money can be borrowed and deployed with returns that will meet certain size and timing assumptions. When those assumptions turn out to be wrong and the profits are delayed or less than anticipated, the burden of that excessive optimism comes home to roost.

   Too much debt stresses cash and cash flow, which ultimately endangers the viability of the business. Interest payments must be made. Loans must be repaid. Covenants must be met. When interest payments, loan repayments, and covenants are missed, management spends its time in workout meetings with the lender instead of running and growing the business.

If the debt is severe enough, the existence of the business is threatened. Understanding the debt structure, interest rates, debt maturities, debt service requirements and capabilities, and robustness of lender relationships is crucial for all business owners. Making sure there are adequate cash reserves to fund future debt repayment obligations is mandatory.

To help me avoid excessive optimism, over-leveraging, and the dreaded dumb tax, I use a simple formula I call the Power of 3. (I elaborate on the formula in Core Discipline #4—Consider 2nd-Order Consequences—in "The 5 Core Disciplines of Thinking" and again in "The 4 Hats of Business.") I am not saying it's perfect, but it has protected me from my tendency toward using emotions and my glands to run my businesses.

a. What's the upside? (I am pretty good at this one, and so are you.)

b. What's the downside? (We rarely think this one through, because we ignore risks.)

c. Can I live with the downside? (Only the pros ask this question, which is why they are rich.)

6. **Excess Capacity Risk:** Like all machines, businesses are comprised of integrated parts. It does no good to have an engine that can go 300 mph if the suspension can only handle 100 mph. The extra 200 mph of horsepower under the hood are a waste. Similarly, every business has underutilized assets or excess production capability that can be made more productive, outsourced, or eliminated from the business's cost or capital structure. Examples might include staff, inventory, excessive receivables, production capability, knowledge, strategic relationships, expertise, office or warehouse space, alliances, etc.

A key component of running the business end of your business is correctly identifying where the business should allocate its resources. If resources are idle or lacking in productivity, a great business Owner will strike immediately and remedy this waste.

The myth that entrepreneurs are risk-takers is misguided. The entrepreneurs you read about in the *Wall Street Journal* and *Forbes* magazine have taken *calculated* risks. They understood what could go wrong, had a "Plan B," and managed their business to minimize the probability and cost in the event of a mistake.

Here it is on a bumper sticker: Minimizing the internal and external risks and how these risks impact the predictability and sustainability of your future stream of earning is critical to the value of your business and your ultimate exitability as an Owner.

Thinking Time

- What are the concentration risks in our business?
- Where are we exposed if we lose a key person or relationship?
- What could disrupt our revenue, customer acquisition, repeat business, or referrals? (Chipotle restaurants and Blue Bell Ice Cream thought this wasn't a risk . . . until it was.)
- What could cause our expenses to dramatically escalate?
- Where are the risks in our business model structure?
- What assumptions are we making about the continuity of our business structure and source(s) of revenue?
- What are the external risks that we are exposed to and how might we best inoculate ourselves from catching whatever "disease" might break out?
- Where have we been overly optimistic with our capital structure and debt load?
- What is the plan if our revenues and cash flow take a 25% hit?
- How much do I need in dry powder (cash reserves) to be able to weather a six- to twelve-month storm?
- Where is the excess capacity in our business? How do we make our "assets" more productive or eliminate some waste/redundancy?

- What really needs to happen to improve the exitability of my business?
- What are the three primary initiatives I must focus on as CEO to maximize the enterprise value?
- If someone offered me an opportunity to buy my business, what price would I pay?
- What can I do to increase that number by 50% in the next twelve months?

NOW . . . Go Think! You will thank me later.

KJC

CHAPTER 41

IT'S NOT ABOUT THE PLAN

I love what Dwight D. Eisenhower said on this subject: "In preparing for battle, I have always found that plans are useless, but planning is indispensable."

I love Mike Tyson's quip even better: "Everyone has a plan until I punch 'em in the nose."

The biggest problem with plans is that they rarely work out the way we envisioned. Certainly, making a plan more detailed does not increase the likelihood that the plan itself is viable, nor does it give us any greater degree of control. To quote another great military strategist, Field Marshal Helmuth Karl Bernhard Graf von Moltke, "No plan survives contact with the enemy." Gilda Radner's *Saturday Night Live* character Roseanne Roseannadanna said it still more succinctly: "It's always something."

The reality is that a plan is a series of assumptions about future events and anticipated activities, which is why plans rarely come off without a hitch. We can't know the future. Either the environment shifts or the activities performed were faulty or inadequate. Our assumptions about both are invariably wrong, and therefore the results ultimately produced are different than anticipated.

So, why do it? Because the value is not in the plan. The value is in the *planning*.

Being intimate with how all the pieces are interconnected and which levers drive specific results is the key to knowing what to adjust when things get off course or delayed.

Among the host of issues critical to planning are:

- understanding your current situation;

- describing the clear outcome desired;

- defining the specific obstacles preventing the attainment of this outcome;

- designing and anticipating the various activities to be performed;

- knowing the environment you are operating in;

- evaluating the competition's strengths and weaknesses;

- studying the consumer/target market's unfulfilled needs and frustrations and identifying the exact problem these specific consumers/target market want solved;

- committing to the promise your brand makes and the messaging you will create; and

- allocating the resources required.

Some Thinking Time sessions, coupled with a firm grasp of each of the above parameters, will dramatically improve your ability to bridge the gulf between an idea and an actual blueprint for the outcomes envisioned. More importantly, your ability to adjust on the fly to achieve the desired outcomes is profoundly enhanced.

Business owners make three big mistakes when it comes to planning:

1. The most common mistake is substituting a description of the destination for a road map—a plan of exactly and specifically how we are going to get from Point A to Point B. ("Generalizations Kill Clarity" puts this in even plainer English.)

2. The second most common mistake is falling in love with the dream—the destination itself. An obsession with the dream obscures your ability to see whether or not there's a demand for

it. (This subject is so important I've dedicated an entire chapter to it, "Dreams and Demand.")

3. The third most common mistake is creating a ten-year plan, which is crazy. It is never really a plan but rather an idea . . . a dream . . . wishful thinking (which usually takes the form of projected hockey-stick growth and profits based on quadrupling customers on a compound basis with no thought to *how* that magic trick is performed). The reality is that too many things are happening way too fast with too many competitors and changes in the environment to predict future financial performance that far in advance. Most business owners I know would be better off with a ten-year commitment than a ten-year "plan."

The value of planning is the clarity of being able to explain your strategy and blueprint to increase your level of financial success in the current environment, which is very different from being able to explain how the current environment has impacted your level of financial success. One is planning and the other is a justification.

Here are some problems with no planning:

- You are in a constant state of reacting to the problem du jour . . . Whack-a-Mole. If you are reacting, you're too late . . . and tired.

- Like Christopher Columbus, you will not know where you are going, where you are when you get there, or where you have been when it's over.

- You have nothing to flicker against to measure your progress, or to measure the changes in the environment and what needs to be adjusted to get back on track.

- This is where budgets enter the conversation. A budget is simply a set of assumptions about the timing and execution of certain activities performed in a certain environment and translating these activities into financial assumptions. The primary reason why all large successful businesses have budgets is to give the management team optics about how the company is performing in comparison to how it was projected to perform. Using these optics, management can now make the necessary course corrections to get back on track.

- You do not know your resource and critical driver interdependencies to be able to make the midcourse correction adjustments necessary to navigate the inevitable storms, detours, roadblocks, and punches in the nose.

- You are executing on an idea if there is no plan, which never ends well. A flurry of tactical activities to move the needle is the formula for drama and chaos.

Edward Deming (the godfather of quality and process management) put it this way: "If you can't describe the plan or the process to achieve that plan, you don't know what you are doing." Smart man.

Here it is on a bumper sticker: If you cannot get clarity on the plan to achieve the outcome, change the outcome. Even with a plan, you probably will not hit the bull's-eye, but at least you will not end up in a graveyard.

Thinking Time

- Am I currently executing an idea or a plan? If it is an idea, what does the plan need to look like?
- Where have I let my ideas become a substitute for my quarterly and annual plans?
- Since a plan is always executable, do I know which actions to perform next week, next month, next quarter to move the needle toward my outcome?
- Does my team know what they are supposed to be doing to help us get from here to there? If so, what is that . . . specifically?
- Where are my current results deviating from my plan and what are the critical driver performance metrics that must be monitored in light of this variance?
- How does my budget vs. actual financial comparison stack up?

- Were there some faulty assumptions in my current plan? Where?
- Was I overly optimistic about the time frames? Where?
- Has the environment changed and thereby rendered my original plan obsolete? If so, where and what needs to be done about it?
- Was the original plan a good one and the problem is a lack of consistent execution? If so, where?
- Where is the gap between my plan and our results a reflection of a mediocre team or weak players?
- Is the team sound but the problem is a lousy culture or a lack of training? Where?
- Maybe the training is good, but the problem is that no one is measuring the critical drivers and taking immediate corrective action? If so, where?
- How do I know which of these might be true and what needs to happen to correct this situation?

NOW . . . Go Think! You will thank me later.
KJC

CHAPTER 42

MY BIGGEST PROBLEM IS . . .

Over the last twenty-five years of advising, coaching, and teaching business owners around the world, I've heard this complaint thousands of times: "My biggest problem is I don't know what I don't know." My response is always the same. "While not knowing what you don't know might be a problem, I seriously doubt it's your biggest problem. A far bigger problem is that you don't do what you do know."

We tend to always be on the lookout for some new, hot idea that will get us from Point A to Point B quicker and easier, with less effort and sweat.

All other things being equal:

- Would you rather have more of something, or less?
- Would you rather have it sooner or later?
- Would you rather have it easier to get, or harder?

I already know your answers. What we have just established is that human nature is to be greedy, impatient, and lazy . . . Not exactly the formula for success and mastery.

When you stop to think about it, what gets us into trouble and causes most of our problems (and dumb tax) is our genetic coding to look for the easiest path to success. Our biggest problems are a result of a never-ending quest to find the path of least resistance instead of a commitment to do whatever it takes to achieve the desired outcome. You can't commit if you are still looking, and most of us are looking for the easier way. We seem to be addicted to "keeping our options open" . . . to find a way that is less painful or requires less sacrifice . . . a way that enables us to be passive and still be rich.

Here it is on a bumper sticker: Everyone wants to go to heaven, no one wants to die. There is no success without sacrifice. (I get on my soapbox in "Something for Nothing . . . *Seriously?*" if you're interested.)

The reality is that most of us would be much farther along if we simply asked ourselves the question, "What can I do today to improve my situation?" and then picked up the shovel and started digging where we are while simultaneously learning new skills and tools. (The chapter "Ordinary Things, Consistently Done, Produce Extraordinary Results!" describes this valuable insight in greater detail.)

Don't get me wrong. The last thing I would ever advise anyone to do is to stop looking for new strategies and distinctions. I read two or three books a week and have for almost thirty years. I attend seminars and listen to audiotapes constantly. My personal library is immense.

But I have also learned that education without execution (i.e., getting things done) is "shelf help." If I don't apply the techniques, strategies, and distinctions I am learning, I will make no forward progress. To achieve my outcomes, I need to get started by doing something. I need to break a sweat. You will find the same principle is true about this book: read it and do the work.

Here it is on a bumper sticker: Being addicted to learning is critical to success . . . but so is being addicted to the business end of a shovel. Problems deferred are problems magnified. (The chapter "Execution" will help you zoom in on your biggest problem—*not doing what you know.*)

Thinking Time

- What decisions have I been postponing in the irrational hope that the problem will somehow resolve itself?
- I am aware there is one primary decision in my business that I have been avoiding, and that this decision is the thing that is holding me back. What do I intend to do about it?
- What is the decision I know I need to make?
- What am I tolerating in my business that is sabotaging my results or that is incongruent with my standards?
- Where am I stuck?
- What have we done in the past that has worked in solving this problem?
- What is my largest competitor doing to address this issue?
- What do I already know that I should be doing but I am not executing . . . or not executing on a consistent basis?
- Where am I paralyzed because I am looking for an easier answer instead of doing what I know?
- Where have I allowed the need for perfect to get in the way of possible?
- What could I do today to improve my situation?
- If what I know is insufficient to making forward progress, what new strategies and skills do I need to learn, who do I need to learn them from, what books do I need to read, or what courses do I need to take?
- Where is my shovel and why am I not using it?

NOW . . . Go Think! You will thank me later.
KJC

CHAPTER 43

OPTIONS ANALYSIS MATRIX

One of my biggest problems is getting clarity about the various choices (options) I have created and which one I should prioritize and execute on.

Like you, I frequently get fuzzy about which of my numerous alternatives is the better course of action. I have found that too many choices is not freedom, it's confusion. I know I don't have the resources to do everything, but what are the guardrails and filters I need to narrow down the field to the best one, given the resources I have and the outcome I am trying to achieve?

I have also learned through the years that it is rare for one choice to be the Holy Grail. Finding the idea or strategy that perfectly solves all my problems and simultaneously requires the least amount of money or effort is impossible.

Here it is on a bumper sticker: All choices require a trade-off and sacrifice. You can have almost anything you want . . . you just can't have everything you want.

The Options Analysis Matrix that follows is designed to give you clarity on possible solutions or decisions available to you by facilitating a side-by-side comparison/ranking based on several fundamental criteria. I have suggested several criteria, but you should feel free to amend or substitute these benchmarks for something more useful if needed.

The key to successful options analysis is to actually see your choices in a comparative format. Trying to weigh the pros and cons of each choice in your head is a fool's game that inevitably leads to a dumb (inferior) choice.

The best way to use this matrix is to keep it simple. For instance, Time might be a certain date in the future or the elapsed number of days or months between now and the anticipated outcome. Effort might be the percentage of your time or hours per week. Money might be the dollar amount. Price Tag or Competence or Risk could be a numerical scale of 1–10. Every category on this matrix will require you to make an estimate. The more you need certainty or exactitude, the harder (and less valuable) this tool will be.

You'll get the highest value from completing the Options Analysis Matrix if you concentrate on these three factors:

- Clarity about what you are optimizing for;
- Brutal honesty;
- Critical thinking.

Notice that the first thing you must obtain is extreme clarity about the outcome you want. Ask yourself the question "What am I optimizing for?" There simply is not a way to evaluate the merits of one option against another option without clarity on the "what" you are trying to achieve.

Candor about resources, time frames, investments, payoffs, and risks is also necessary. Lying to yourself or using wishful thinking as your filter will render the Options Analysis Matrix useless. This level of honesty is frequently accessed with the help of a third party (a Board of Directors or business coach).

Working through the merits of various options will require being thoughtful about your assumptions and the risks embedded in each option. You must carefully and critically think through all aspects of each option available.

The upper part of this matrix (Time, Effort, Money, Price Tag, Competence, Risk, Acceptable Consequences) is the input side of the

OPTIONS ANALYSIS MATRIX					
We are optimizing for:					
	Option #1	Option #2	Option #3	Option #4	Option #5
Time					
Effort					
Money					
Price Tag					
Competence					
Risk					
Acceptable Consequences					

	Equals	Equals	Equals	Equals	Equals
How Much Money					
When / Date					

Ranking					

Time = Elapsed calendar time from today?

Effort = Hours (or percentage) of *your* time involved?

Money = Resource investment required? (People or money)

Price Tag = What activity must either stop or start? What will get sacrificed by choosing this option? (*Hint:* It is out of your comfort zone.)

Competence = Where does it fall within your execution intelligence and existing expertise?

Risk = Probability of Success & Cost of Failure?

Acceptable Consequences = Is the price of failure worth the risk of reward? Is the juice worth the squeeze?

Equals

How Much Money = What is the monetary payoff of this option?

When / Date = Realistically, when will the results or payoff most likely occur?

Rank = Based on all the factors and considerations above, including your relative subjective weightings, on a scale of 1–10, how do these options stack up?

equation. The lower part of this matrix (How Much Money, When/Date) is the output.

Ranking is performed after the matrix has been completed and is based on *all* the factors included in your Options Analysis Matrix. The ranking will be highly subjective, based on the relative importance or weighting you place on the various categories.

A word of caution: Simply summing the totals to give you certainty or a precise formula or a course of action is stupid. Not all the input factors can be equally weighted. Instead, use the Options Analysis Matrix as it was intended—a tool to support your thinking about the viability and relative attractiveness of the various options available to you and your business.

Thinking Time

- What major outcome am I optimizing for? (Specificity is my friend.)
- What are the various options I have created or found?
- For each of the options I have created:
  - What is the estimated amount of time between now and the attainment of the outcome?
  - How many hours (or what percentage of my time) would be required?
  - How much money (investment) would be required?
  - Which current activities would be reduced or stopped to be able to add this option to our execution agenda? (What must be sacrificed?)
  - Do we have the expertise and execution intelligence (competence) to successfully perform the tasks required?
  - What is the probability of failure? (If this option fails, what is the financial and lost opportunity cost?)
  - Is the price of failure worth the risk?
  - If this option succeeds, what is the monetary payoff?

- When (date or lapsed time from today) will we receive the payoff from executing on this option?
- In evaluating all the various input and output factors about each option and comparing these various data points, which option appears to be the most viable and attractive?
- Are there any input categories (variables) that deserve to be weighted differently that might skew my analysis and thinking?

NOW . . . Go Think! You will thank me later.

KJC

CHAPTER 44

CAUSE AND EFFECT

Everyone I know would love to be rich, healthy, fit, and in a wonderful relationship. These are effects . . . and they are easy to fall in love with. But if the key to wealth, health, and relationships was to be in love with the end result, then everyone would already have these outcomes, and they don't, so it's not.

As you have already discovered in your life, the critical distinction is not falling in love with the effect (outcome). It's consistently executing on the cause.

Here it is on a bumper sticker: Whenever the effect is missing, so is the cause. Execute and manage the cause and the effect will take care of itself.

So, whatever it is you want in your life, check to see if the cause is in place to produce the desired effect. If it is, then it's just a matter of time and consistent, daily execution until you see the effects show up.

Remember, cause and effect are not necessarily closely linked in time. It might take thousands of hours of practice to produce certain results. Other results can be produced in much less time. It depends on the outcome and the quality/intensity of the practice.

The key to success is consistency of execution on the right things at the right time. Consistently executing the wrong things will not deliver the outcomes you want. Inconsistently executing the right things will also fail to deliver the desired end result. And few things are more common than doing the right thing at the wrong time. A lot of variables, right?

Think of causes as critical drivers and effects as key performance indicators (KPIs). Stepping on the bathroom scale is a KPI. Diet and exercise are critical drivers. Measure and manage the diet and exercise, and there is probably very little reason to step on the scales.

No question KPIs are powerful tools, but they tell you what has happened *after the fact* (the bathroom scale) and are not predictive of what needs to change to create different results in the future. The predictor of your weight is directly correlated to your diet and exercise.

Measuring the critical drivers is the *only* way to create *sustainable* business success. (This is so critical I've written an entire chapter about it: "What Gets Measured Is . . .".) Most business owners just measure the end results, or KPIs. A KPI might be sales, profits, or gross margins.

If you want to step up your optics for better decision making as well as your level of business mastery, you must identify and measure your critical drivers, too.

Measuring and monitoring your critical driver activities gives you the ability to understand what is happening in your business *before* seeing the financial statements at the end of the month, quarter, or year. They are an early warning system that illuminates where you might be veering slightly off course and gives you enough information so you can do something about it before the situation becomes a problem. (For more insights on critical drivers, see my book *The Ultimate Blueprint*.)

Here it is on a bumper sticker: The hard part is not envisioning the outcome or setting the goal. It's figuring out what needs to change and consistently executed to reach this outcome. If you know what needs to change and get executed, you know what needs to be measured. These are your critical drivers. Execute on the critical drivers and close the gap. (Take another look at Core Discipline #2—Separate the Problem from the Symptom—in "The 5 Core Disciplines of Thinking.")

Thinking Time

- What are the outcomes (effects) I want that are still undelivered?
- If my outcomes are missing or the gap is not closing, what are the causes that are missing?
- Is the problem that we are inconsistently executing on the right things? If so, how do we tighten this up?
- I need to reexamine my desired outcomes (goals) from the viewpoint of cause and effect. Has my progress or momentum stalled because I am not seeing instantaneous results?
- Where am I running the wrong direction enthusiastically?
- Is there an obstacle in my way that requires a new solution and different execution?
- What is stopping me from doing my job?
- How would the person I want to be do the thing I am about to do?
- What is my level of intensity and will this level of engagement produce my desired effects?
- What am I executing that used to work but is not the right strategy in this environment?
- What do I need to stop doing and what do I need to start doing?
- When I have a bad month financially, what are the three to five things that should have happened that didn't happen? What are the three to five things that did happen that shouldn't have happened? These are my critical drivers.
- What needs to change to create the outcome/standard we have set and what will I measure to ensure consistent performance on these critical drivers?
- What is the specific measurable standard of performance we need to achieve for each critical driver to ensure we are moving toward the desired outcome (effect)?
- How frequently do these critical drivers need to be measured and reported?
- What is the dashboard I will use that provides me with the optics necessary to understand our performance and take corrective action?

- How do I best engage my team in the process of measuring, monitoring, and correcting on each critical driver standard?
- How do I give my team ownership of their critical drivers?

NOW . . . Go Think! You will thank me later.

KJC

CHAPTER 45

WHAT GETS MEASURED IS . . .

Serena Williams, Jordan Spieth, and Warren Buffett have one thing in common: They are measuring freaks.

Measuring is the primary, fundamental tool used by all pros and experts to excel and win the game. (The previous chapter, "Cause and Effect," speaks about the value of measuring your business's critical drivers.) Here's why:

- It focuses management's attention on what's important.

- It monitors performance to ensure improvement.

- It highlights the gaps (weaknesses) in performance between where you are and where you expected to be so that the appropriate area gets the remedial action.

- It forces you to face reality and see what needs to be changed, corrected, or improved.

Here are a few tricks to effective measuring:

- Have a standard (outcome) to strive for.

- Have a standard to use as a comparison tool to see where you are vs. where you want to be.

- Measure and monitor the trends. Are things getting better or worse and do you know why?

- Measure the critical drivers, not the trivial many. Measuring more things is not useful. Measuring the right things is.

- Frequency is key. Stepping on the bathroom scales every 10 minutes is stupid. So is stepping on the scales only once each year. Different drivers will require different frequencies. Balance sheets are monitored monthly, but cash is frequently measured daily. Profits are also measured monthly, but revenue is often measured daily too.

- It does no good to measure and then fail to communicate your findings to the appropriate people. Often this requires having a hard conversation. That's okay, because nothing can change until the unsaid is spoken.

Here it is on a bumper sticker:
- What gets measured is what gets done.
- What gets measured is what gets managed.
- What gets measured and reported can improve exponentially.

Thinking Time
- Where are my results weakest? What keeps me up at night and what am I measuring to identify the problems and improve the situation?
- What are the three to five critical drivers I need to measure to ensure the progress I want?
- What is the standard (specifically) of each critical driver and are these standards clearly communicated to the person responsible for achieving them?
- What are the hard conversations I need to have based on the results we are getting, so we can correct and improve?

- Based on our measuring, what is the training needed to raise our performance and improve our results? (After all, if they can train a polar bear to ride a tricycle, how hard can it be to train my people to do their job?)
- Where (exactly) is our consistency of execution deficient and what needs to be done about that problem?
- What is the dashboard I need to create so that my measuring, critical drivers, and standards are all in one place and easy for me to digest?
- Based on the optics I receive from my measuring and dash-boards, where have we settled for mediocre and average instead of demanding excellence?
- What (specifically) needs to change to hit our standards and produce excellence?

NOW . . . Go Think! You will thank me later.
KJC

CHAPTER 46

THE GREAT QUESTION

It is so easy to major in minor things. We have a tendency to find and work on the projects we can easily or quickly get knocked out instead of the harder, more impactful projects that will require much more time and effort but will yield significantly greater long-term dividends. (Read "The 3 Pillars of Success" and "The Triangle of Death" if you doubt me on this.)

The "easy," quick-fix projects make us feel like we are doing something, even if what we are doing is not particularly additive or productive. More often than not, these quickie and urgent projects are reactionary and tactical vs. anticipatory and strategic.

No wonder we're tired; we are reacting to the environment instead of planning and creating it. It does no good to touch a thousand different things each quarter if none of them move.

Here it is on a bumper sticker: All activities consume resources. You can't shift priorities without simultaneously shifting resources.

Without prioritization of the outcomes there is no prioritization of activities; therefore, resources get consumed in a frantic attempt to do everything instead of the most meaningful thing. Mismanaging this relationship between priorities and resources has filled many business graveyards. Multitasking is stupid at the CEO/Owner/Board level of a business.

In my Board of Directors, our tradition is to plan and think in terms of one "major" and two or three "minors" for the upcoming quarter. (See appendix 2 for more information on our Board of Directors for business owners.) A major priority is a very important outcome or project that is being elevated off our To-Do list and will now receive enough calendar time, bandwidth, and resources to make measurable progress. It is *the* thing that, if focused on and accomplished, would have the greatest significant impact on the business in the coming ninety days. A minor is important (not as important as a major), but still qualifies for elevated time, focus, and attention.

My experience has been that figuring out the most important outcome or project is actually one of the hardest parts of this exercise. We tend to default into thinking that lots of things are important and that narrowing our priorities down to just a few is impossible or unrealistic, given all the stuff that needs attention. Let me assure you it's not. My rule is: Start fewer things, finish more things.

It is remarkable how powerful clarity of outcomes and deliverables can be at generating momentum, focus, and results. (And minimizing the need to respond to every kitten scratching at your screen door.)

Remember this critical distinction when you are setting priorities (and shifting resources accordingly): Vague, glossy majors or minors are useless. "I will improve the revenues in the next quarter" is a meaningless statement, because there are no metrics or specifics attached to it that show how the outcome will be achieved. (See "Generalizations Kill Clarity" for more details about this subject.)

The great question is: "What am I optimizing for?" In other words, what is the one major that, if accomplished, would have the most significant impact on my business?

Thinking Time

- What am I optimizing for?
- What one meaningful, specific outcome, if I achieved it, would have a significant positive impact on my business?

- What are the specific obstacles standing in my way of making measurable progress on this outcome?
- What specific activities must I prioritize to make measurable progress toward this outcome?
- What resources would need to be acquired or reconfigured to move the needle on this priority?
- What are the three most significant things I could do this week that would kick the can and close the gap by moving me closer to my major priority?
- What are three things I would need to stop doing to make room for this major priority?
- How do I regain control of my calendar and minimize the "got-a-minute" interruptions that are sabotaging my time?
- How much time should I spend thinking about what I need to prioritize and spend time on?
- If I am raising my standards by prioritizing my majors, activities, and deliverables, how might I enroll my senior leadership team in this process as well? (You will be stunned by their accountability and the progress people can make when they have clarity about their majors and minors and what *they* are optimizing for.)

NOW . . . Go Think! You will thank me later.
KJC

CHAPTER 47

ADVICE FROM THE CHAIRMAN OF THE BOARD

So let me put this book into a lengthy bumper sticker for you. I am repeating myself now, because this final chapter is a summation of many of the critical ideas I have discussed throughout *The Road Less Stupid*. Don't be tempted to ignore this last chapter. It has some equally great ideas for your consideration during your next Thinking Time session.

It turns out that the key to getting rich is to avoid doing stupid things. The vast majority of dumb tax in both of our lives is a direct result of emotional and optimistic decisions.

The key point I have made in each chapter is the importance of getting clarity by asking really good questions. The questions at the end of each chapter have been designed to force you to really think for a change instead of emotionally reacting and defaulting to the most obvious "best idea" available in the moment.

Here it is on a bumper sticker: Operators react and sweat. Owners think and plan.

The player on the field in a football game must get psychologically jacked up and mentally erase any doubts about the ultimate domination by his team over the opponent. Mental belief and optimism are critical to high performance on the gridiron.

The pregame and halftime locker room pep talks are designed to get the *players* into a "peak state" so they will perform at the highest level. In a football game, the players are the doers, the performers, and they must get amped up to excel at their job. Igniting this excitement and passion is a critical ingredient to ensure their success on the field. An Operator of a business is fueled by this same exuberance, hubris, and extreme confidence.

The Owner of the football team, however, should never be one of the people sitting in the locker room listening to the halftime pep talk in an effort to decide whether or not to add fifteen new luxury box suites to the stadium next year.

The Owner of the team must be strategic (not emotionally tactical) in his thinking. He must consider the overall game plan, the key personnel on the bench, and who is injured or has recently struggled to perform, as well as the weaknesses on the opponent's bench.

The Owner must mentally plan for an astonishing number of hypothetical what-if scenarios that might arise during the game. And this doesn't include the stadium naming rights, the number of season tickets sold, whether the cash flow of the business is sufficient to meet payroll this month, how much money is being returned to the investors for the risk they took, and all the things that could go wrong that would eat his leg off.

If the Owner of the team made his decisions by first sitting through a pep rally from a motivational coach, we would have a very enthusiastic Owner with no money. No exceptions. Owners and members of a Board of Directors do not work themselves into an emotional frenzy prior to a Board meeting. Ever!

Most business owners and entrepreneurs experience a major shock when confronted with the advice and counsel of a true Board of Directors. A Board does not care how optimistic you are or how much you believe in yourself or whether or not your product is your passion or life's purpose. A great Board knows that exciting stories, inclusion on the list of Inc. 500 fastest-growing companies, first-mover advantage, Entrepreneur of the Year awards, and projected hockey stick returns are the breakfast of the membership director of a fraternity, not a seasoned CEO. Check your medals and your ego at the door. Business is personal, but not emotional.

At the Owner and Board levels, success is not contingent on excessive enthusiasm on the field but rather by the quality of the planning, preparation, risk assessment, and risk mitigation strategies. Thinking about 2nd-order consequences and unrealistic assumptions is mandatory. Skepticism and thinking are your best friends when sitting in the Owner's box. (See "The 5 Core Disciplines of Thinking," especially Core Discipline #4—Consider the 2nd-Order Consequences.)

Andy Grove, founder and former CEO and Chairman of Intel, said it best: "Only the paranoid survive."

Here is the distinction:

When a group of operators get together, it's called a convention. You will have a great time, everyone will yuk it up, party all night, give each other awards, plaques, and standing ovations for being so successful. This stuff might massage your ego and make you feel good, but none of it will make you rich. Attempting to make a business decision while wearing the Artist or Operator hat will result in stupid (see "The 4 Hats of Business").

When a group of business owners get together, it's called a Board meeting. The goal of a Board is to help you think through the risks and possible 2nd-order consequences, thereby minimizing the likelihood of you doing something stupid.

Every great Board of Directors knows that

- The single most toxic poison in business is excessive emotion. Emotions and intellect work inversely. As I said at the start of *The Road Less Stupid*, when emotion goes up, intellect goes down.

- Every business is just one bad decision away from a financial disaster. Look no farther than Lehman Brothers: 130 years old; $1.4 trillion in assets; gone in 90 days because of one stupid decision . . . and numerous unexamined assumptions.

- Over the long term, the amount of net worth on the balance sheet or money in the bank is determined more by the number and size of the losses incurred and less by the number or size of the winners hit. There is always uncertainty and, therefore, risks. In business, an addiction to certainty is rarely your friend. Assessing and controlling risk (which is paramount to financial success) is only possible by thinking through key risk related questions:

- What are the risks we are facing? Really!
- What is the probability of these risks occurring?
- How costly are these risks should they occur?
- How can we control or mitigate the probability or the cost?
- Where have we substituted optimism for risk assessment in our business and thinking?
- What assumptions have I made about our future that might not be true, and if they ultimately proved to be untrue, what contingency plans do I need to develop today to ensure survival if I am wrong?
- Where have I let my emotions and need for more interfere with my judgment?

What we achieved in the past is a poor predictor of what we will achieve in the future. I am certain Netscape, Atari, AltaVista, Polaroid, and JC Penny would agree with me that the rules and the environment are always changing. People who are impressed with their prior success or who crave fame and applause rarely make the changes required to be relevant in the future. Leadership requires humility. No humility, no learning.

A great Board will not agree with you so that you will feel good, nor are they willing to become one of your groupie fans sitting in the stands enthusiastically cheering you on in the misguided belief that if they would just cheer louder, you will win the game.

A wall of accolades for past success and pictures with famous people are wonderful for the ego (I call this the "I love me . . . look how great I am" wall), but they do nothing to put money into your pocket or drive sustainable business success. Use a Thinking Time session or two in deep thought about the future and where you are being lulled to sleep by past success:

- Where have I extrapolated past performance as a predictor for future results?

- Where have we confused applause for past performance with future financial success?

- Where have we allowed our past success to lull us into believing we are bulletproof?

- What business decisions do we need to make to ensure our future viability?

- Given the current marketplace landscape, which part of our business needs to be reinvented?

- Where are our results diminishing even though we are still doing what we used to? In light of this assessment, what needs to change?

Being aggressive with expansion is always risky, especially when a stable foundation is not in place, the management team is not solid, or you are relying on the capital structure (excessive debt) to produce the returns required. Doubling the horsepower of the engine in your car or substituting rocket fuel for your unleaded gas will not enable the car to go two times faster. Scaling mediocrity produces bigger piles of mediocrity, not success. Always optimize first.

All business owners want to grow, but few have the discipline to create a sound platform for that growth prior to pouring in the jet fuel. Contrary to popular opinion, the solution to the vast majority of business problems has little to do with the size of the top line.

Here it is on a bumper sticker: Growth is what you say "yes" to. Success is what you say "no" to. The hardest thing in business is figuring out what to say "no" to. Warren Buffett said it best: "The difference between successful people and very successful people is that very successful people say no to almost everything."

Expanding prematurely is a prescription for disaster, especially if the expansion is funded by excessive debt. Leverage magnifies the results but does nothing to change the fundamental risk characteristics of the investment.

One final point on this: Scaling a hand-crank process does not result in more bottom-line profits. It results in more "crankers." Scaling when the lug nuts on a Formula One race car are not tight or there's not a process/culture to keep them tight results in wrecks, not success. Automating, systematizing, or scaling weakness is the foundation for misery and failure. Before you stomp on the gas, think through the following questions to make sure the chassis, springs, and shocks can withstand the torque:

- When I take a hard look at my expansion and growth plans, do we have a base that is rock-solid, or are we relying on a rising tide and calm waters?

- Does my team have the bandwidth required to continue to do the job they are currently doing plus handle the incremental growth and new customers I am projecting? (See "Indigestion (1+1 ≠ 2)" for more on this issue.)

- Where have I allowed our enthusiasm for our ideas to be a substitute for a solid, executable plan?

- The first step in self-delusion is denial. Where are we running with scissors? (My observations in "Creating Enterprise Value" are particularly germane in this regard.)

- Risks and facts don't cease to exist just because I ignore them, and thinking that risk is under control is the greatest risk there is. Risk analysis requires extreme humility (overconfidence is the enemy) and the courage to admit not knowing what you don't know. What are the Top 10 risks we are facing and what can we do to mitigate the cost or probability of each risk identified? ("Not All Risks Are Created Equal" takes a thorough look at accessing and managing risk.)

We all have limited resources. It is impossible to attempt to do everything we think of or take advantage of every opportunity that presents itself. As CEO, your job is to carefully and selectively prioritize the few key strategies and initiatives that will optimize the financial performance of the business while simultaneously leveraging the resources available.

Prioritize the things that aren't in place but, if they were, would make the biggest difference to the business. (Both "The Great Question" and "A CEO Should *Never* Delegate . . ." gave you solid advice about how, when, and what to prioritize.)

- What are we optimizing for?
- What is my major outcome?
- Where have we spread ourselves too thin by attempting to do too much?
- Which activities or initiatives need to be stopped or paused so that we can concentrate on the most critical strategies and stabilize/grow our business?
- What are the underutilized resources in my business and how can I best put those resources (strengths) to work?

It takes courage and trust for a CEO to engage with a Board of Directors. Sometimes even great CEOs will be tempted to sugarcoat or disguise the issues in an attempt to appear capable and strong.

Courage is a key ingredient for leadership. In fact, every failure of leadership has at its root a lack of courage. Courage to

- say what needs to be said;
- ask for advice;
- admit mistakes and errors in judgment;
- make the difficult decisions and have the hard conversations;
- listen with the intent to understand, not the intent to justify or reply;
- initiate change; and
- face reality.

I lacked courage forty years ago with my first Board of Directors. I was afraid to ask for advice because I erroneously believed that exposing my doubts and anxieties were signs of incompetence.

But I had it all wrong. The Board meetings weren't all about *me*. They were all about the business. And it was crucial that anything and everything that could possibly have an impact on the life, the survival of the business needed to be brought to the table. I've since realized these truths about the necessity of communicating with a Board:

- A Board of Directors is neither a cheerleader nor a critic. Board members are "partners" and collaborators in designing success. A Board acts as an advisor and counselor for a CEO. Board members poke, ask questions, and prod as they look for icebergs, unexamined assumptions, and wishful thinking.

- A Board never thinks about opportunities without simultaneously thinking about the risks, probabilities, downsides, costs, and trade-offs associated with those opportunities.

- A Board knows that what kills the business is not missing an opportunity but rather unseen risks. Boards think in terms of 2nd-order consequences and ensuring survival (in the event things turn ugly) rather than a financial bonanza if everything goes as planned). (Reread Core Discipline #4—Consider 2nd-Order Consequences in "The 5 Core Disciplines of Thinking" to appreciate the importance of this point.)

- A Board of Directors knows that a plan that requires you to dodge all the bullets to be successful is not a plan; it's a hallucination.

Use these Thinking Time questions to get greater clarity about some decisions you need to make for your business:

- Who do I have around me that I can count on to question my assumptions and ask me the tough questions?

- Who will tell me what I don't want to hear?

- Who on my team will tell me "no"?

- Where are we relying on a perfect environment or flawless execution to create the success we are predicting?

- Where am I allowing a lack of courage to dictate my decisions?

I have found in my forty-five-year business career that the majority of my mistakes (losses) were a result of unexamined assumptions and tolerating an inferior team/culture that did not execute consistently. I sometimes relied too heavily on the brilliance of my idea. I did not pay close enough attention to the risks, which created even more risk because I went all in when I should have folded or checked.

I erroneously believed that the higher the risk, the higher the reward, which is just plain stupid. The correct statement is this: The higher the risk, the greater the likelihood of a loss, not a reward.

I mistook luck for skill and extrapolated my past performance as an accurate predictor of my future success. I did not surround myself with smart people who were strong enough to disagree with me.

My fatal flaw was the illusion that I am somehow special and could beat the odds with my sheer determination, sweat, and brainpower. Dumb!

Here it is on a bumper sticker: Business is an intellectual sport. We make the mistake of believing we can somehow get rich or become successful by

- being passionate enough;
- wanting it desperately enough;
- visualizing it long enough;
- believing that we are entitled enough;
- being talented enough; and/or
- working hard enough.

It doesn't work that way. Passion and desire might produce a willingness to persist, but they do not teach the skills and tools to create the success. The advice (and book) *Do What You Love and the Money Will Follow* is as stupid as it is destructive. This is analogous to saying, "Eat What You Want and Be Skinny."

Doing what you love might make you feel fulfilled. It might make a great hobby or pastime. You might feel energized and excited. You might make a huge contribution, but simply loving to *do* something will not create business or financial success.

On the other hand, hating what you do is not a prescription for success either. Don't miss my point here: I am not arguing for or against being passionate about what you do; I am just pointing out that passion alone is not the one-trick pony for business success.

Sustainably successful business *Owners* play the game with their heads, not their emotions. It's chess, not checkers.

Investing is about the future, and the future is unknown (by *everyone*). Believing with all your heart, staring in the mirror, telling yourself how special you are, and mustering all the certainty you can access that the future is a sure thing do not cause it to be so . . . ever. Do not make the mistake of confusing certainty with clarity; they are two different things!

The people who sustainably win at business excel at sorting out and managing the risks. They do not have their lips securely attached to their own exhaust pipes to keep themselves jacked up emotionally on hopium, excitement, and a naive conviction that if they are just certain enough, they can achieve their dreams through sheer willpower, passion, and belief.

Here is the real "secret": The chance of success goes up when you think, plan, consistently execute the right things, and worry about the possibility of loss.

NOW . . . Go Think! You will thank me later.
KJC

CHAPTER 48

ONE LAST THING

We erroneously believe that getting more stuff will make us "more happy," yet as the great Swiss mathematician Daniel Bernoulli observed, "The utility resulting from any small increase in wealth will be inversely proportional to the quality of goods previously possessed."

In plain English, this simply means that the second candy bar is never as satisfying as the first one . . . and the tenth candy bar is even less so. An extra billion dollars to Bill Gates is a rounding error and therefore meaningless, not because a billion dollars is a small amount of money but because he already has so many of them.

Part of the problem seems to be how we casually use the words "pleasure" and "happy" interchangeably. The reality is that they are two different things. It's human nature to desire sensual pleasures long after they cease to provide the initial thrill (or satisfaction) of the first encounter. The misguided belief is that more pleasure will make us "more happy."

Furthermore, the pleasure we first experienced is mislabeled as "happy" because it made us feel good. It should have been labeled as "pleasurable," which is what it really was. The unbridled pursuit of pleasure can easily be transformed into debilitating habits and destructive addictions . . . which ultimately don't make us happy either.

Not only do we tend to mislabel our experiences; to find out how we are doing, we constantly compare ourselves to others and inevitably find ourselves deficient. Someone always seems to have more. In an effort to feel good about ourselves and our ranking, we think the goal must be more, even though what we have is beyond most people's wildest dreams.

If the world were a village of a thousand people:

- 350 are malnourished.
- 330 live in a shantytown (with no running water or central sewage disposal).
- 250 are illiterate (they can't read or write at a first-grade level).
- The median income is $3.30/day.
- 10 make more than $34,000/year (the top 1%).

We feel we don't measure up because we make the fatal mistake of only measuring "up" without the perspective of looking around to see where we actually fit in the grand scheme of things.

Some people will have more than we do, but the majority of people on the planet would consider our nightmare their fantasy. It's easy to be unhappy with my old pair of Nikes until I meet the man with no feet. Besides, it's impossible to be content if I am constantly comparing. True satisfaction comes from advancement and progress, not comparisons.

The mistaken belief that more will make us happy is why we often feel dissatisfied when we reach a desired goal or target. We were expecting happy, instead we got success. Once again, two different things.

Pleasure is a result of stimulating our senses. Happiness, on the other hand, is only available through gratitude. It is gratitude that forces you to focus on the present and not the regrets of the past and the fears of the future. In the present, all is well.

Success is the result of getting more of what you want and rarely creates either happiness or fulfillment. Fulfillment is only available by giving what you've got.

The hero's journey can certainly include pleasure and great success. But the true triumph of happiness and fulfillment is found through gratitude and contribution. William Arthur Ward said it best: "Feeling gratitude and not expressing it is like wrapping a present and not giving it."

At the end of my life, I will only ask three questions:

1. Is the world a better place because of me?
2. Who loved me and who did I love?
3. Was my life congruent with my beliefs? (Which is the ultimate definition of integrity.)

Here it is on a bumper sticker: Pleasure is about stimulating the senses. Happiness is found by being grateful for what I've got. Success is getting what I want. Fulfillment is giving what I've got.

The Road Less Stupid was inspired by my desire to give what I got, and I am grateful for the opportunity you have given me to serve you in your pursuit of success. The truth is, I am the beneficiary of the long hours and many months consumed in this thinking and writing process. Fulfillment seems to work that way.

I am grateful you chose to invest your time with me and this book. Reading it was the easy part. Like all books, *The Road Less Stupid* will only be meaningful if you do the work, which in this case means scheduling Thinking Time sessions and asking the right questions.

NOW . . . Go Think! You will thank me later.
KJC

BUMPER STICKERS, REMINDERS, WORDS OF CAUTION, HINTS & NEVER FORGETS

THE DREADED DUMB TAX

- It turns out that the key to getting rich (and staying that way) is to avoid doing stupid things. I don't need to do more smart things. I just need to do fewer dumb things. I need to avoid making emotional decisions and swinging at bad pitches. I need to think!

- All my problems started out as a good idea, and all those "good" ideas were emotionally justifiable at the time. Not only that, my current financial condition represents my very best "thinking." Yours does, too.

- What sabotages our dreams and causes most of our problems (and ensuing dumb tax) is our excessive optimism and emotional belief in magic pills, secret formulas, and financial tooth fairies. (All balloons look good when they are filled with hot air.) Dumb!

- Emotions and intellect work inversely. When emotions go up, intellect goes down. Optimism is a deadly emotion in the business world. Warren Buffett said it best: "Optimism is the enemy of the rational investor."

- There are no secrets . . . just stuff you haven't learned yet.

THE DISCIPLINE OF THINKING TIME

- Find the Unasked Question—Create a question that will result in clarity and generate better choices.
- Separate the Problem from the Symptom—Identify the real obstacle that is blocking my progress.
- Check Assumptions—Differentiate the facts from the story I am spinning.
- Consider 2nd-Order Consequences—Clarify the risks and the possibility/cost of being wrong.
- Create the Machine—Create the executable plan and identify the resources (people and money) required to solve the real (core) problem and make forward progress.

THE 5 CORE DISCIPLINES OF THINKING

- Having the right answer is smart. Having the right question is genius. Or, as Peter Drucker said, "Most serious mistakes are not being made as a result of wrong answers. The truly dangerous thing is asking the wrong question."
- The key to defining the root problem is discovering the obstacle (it resides in the gap) that is impeding your progress from here to there. It is the obstacle that is the problem, not the dissatisfaction with your current circumstances!
- Building a machine for the problem that isn't and expecting forward progress is delusional.
- If we misdiagnose or mislabel the problem, we will gravitate toward designing solutions and building machines for the symptoms (aka

"the problem that isn't") and this is a prescription for frustration and failure.

- Few things are worse than running the wrong direction enthusiastically. Misdiagnosing the problem or working on the wrong priorities results in a dumb tax!

- What none of us see are the assumptions we make about the problem we have, the solution we create, or the opportunity in front of us. The reality is that virtually all my dumb tax could have been avoided if I had just questioned a couple of obvious assumptions prior to pulling the trigger.

- Stupid in small things, stupid in big things.

- We only have a choice about the decision we are about to make, not the consequences. An important decision that does not identify the possible risks as well as the probability and costs of failure is a decision with a high likelihood of creating drama. The problem with drama is that it always costs money.

- Risks don't cease to exist just because you ignore them, and neither do facts. An honest assessment of what could go wrong, the probability of it going off the rails, and the cost in the event of failure are fundamental to minimizing your dumb tax.

- Thinking about 2nd-order consequences minimizes the probability of a double bogey. Mistakes are inevitable, but double bogeys are usually avoidable.

- Shoes that don't fit are not a bargain at any price. A good idea that can't be executed is a bad idea.

- Ultimately, the problem gets addressed or solved as a result of a machine that will move me from Point A (where I am) to Point B (where I want to go). The expectation is that the new machine will produce an output that improves my situation, closes the gap, and moves me closer to the desired outcome.

- Regardless of the change, management must shift priorities if the new solution has a shot at being effective. Changes in priorities are always accompanied by changes in the allocation of resources. The vast majority of solutions (machines) fail to produce the anticipated outcomes because management is unclear about the required shifts in focus, human capital, and money.

- Measurement is THE key to sustainability and a culture of accountability.

THINKING TIME: THE PROCESS

- Designing a Thinking Time process that works for you will be no different than figuring out any other ritual you want to create. The time of day, the best location, and the optimum duration are all discovered through practice and experimentation until you have created a Thinking Time process that best supports your outcomes. The key here is to obsess about obtaining the outcomes and not about finding the perfect process!

- Fundamentally, Thinking Time is a structured process that enables me to minimize the risks, identify the opportunities, and maximize the results. That is a pretty high return for a very low-cost investment.

MMM . . . KOOL-AID

- Learning doesn't happen until something changes.

- Business is complex and the future is unknown. Tactical solutions, simplistic formulas, and generalized answers tend to cripple rather than enhance success. No one has all the answers and nobody can predict the future, including me. Whatever you do, don't drink my Kool-Aid, either. On the other hand, don't ignore what I'm saying. Do some independent thinking for a change. Just because someone has written a book doesn't mean he knows what he's talking about. The same holds true for me.

- Be careful who you take advice from. Are they really an expert, or just someone with an opinion and a publisher? Be suspicious of one-size-fits-all solutions. Your situation is likely to be unique and require some serious brainpower to sort out the core problems and possible solutions. Be distrustful of advisors who predict the future. (As a Wall Street sage has quipped, "The reason God made economists is to make astrologers look good.")

- Hubris, arrogance, and self-confidence on steroids are typically the breakfast of failure, not success.

- Consultants have a recipe. Masters have a cookbook!

THE 4 HATS OF BUSINESS

- If your dream is to become rich in *business*, then mastering *business* skills is compulsory. Notice I did not say, "Improving your product or becoming a better plumber is compulsory." There's a big difference between winning the gold medal as the best plumber in the world (artistic and operational achievement) and winning the gold medal of making $1,000,000/year of bottom line profit as the Owner of a plumbing business (business success).

- Believing passion and operational excellence will trump business skills and risk assessment is a guaranteed prescription for a breathtaking dumb tax.

- The victim mentality of the what-you-see-is-what-you-get worldview is the perfect excuse to let you off the hook for taking responsibility for your business's outcomes and results. Don't let it. If you want business success, then learn the necessary business skills and tools. There is no such thing as a rich victim.

- Unfortunately, growth and control work inversely. The more growth you desire, the less control you can have (and vice versa).

- The majority of dumb taxes incurred are a direct result of having only one voice in the conversation when the original decision was made. Adding experienced, wise, thoughtful, trustworthy voices to the conversation exposes risks, curtails faulty assumptions, and minimizes stupid.

CULTURE IS KING (YOU GET WHAT YOU TOLERATE)

- The key to a great culture is creating and fostering a never-ending conversation about the "rules of the game." The rules define the boundaries or guardrails so that everyone knows exactly how to act, how to communicate, and how to treat each other. Culture, not a value statement, is the key to high performance and becoming the employer of choice. (Enron's Value Statement was Respect, Integrity, Communication, Excellence. A plaque on the wall is not a substitute for culture, and neither are nap rooms.)

- Anyone who says customers are #1 has lost their mind! Employees are #1. Employees are the source of all value creation. Culture (not jelly beans in the kitchen) is the source for engaged, turned-on employees. Show me a disinterested employee and I'll show you a lousy culture, a weak leader, and a poor customer experience.

- When you're about to initiate a cultural shift, be aware of these three common culture saboteurs:

  - Iceberg #1: Deciding to change the culture within your business is not an initiative for the weak of heart or uncommitted.

  - Iceberg #2: There is always at least one person on a team who thinks he is immune to the culture transformation conversation.

  - Iceberg #3: An unenforced rule is not a rule; it's a suggestion.

- The reason we hesitate to have the hard conversations is because we don't care enough. If you truly cared enough, you would say what needs to be said. After all, how else are they going to improve and maximize their potential? Let me remind you that nothing can change until the unsaid is spoken.

GENERALIZATIONS KILL CLARITY

- Generalizations kill clarity. Clarity equals power. Power is the ability to act. Whenever there is weak, ineffective, or no action, it is usually a result of a lack of clarity and/or accountability. (A Board of Directors is great at filling this role.)

- Glossy and fluffy are always safe (and always produce mediocrity). Specifics and accountability require courage. A plan without specificity of deliverables and dates is a fantasy. Accountability should never be feared; it is the mother of great.

A CEO SHOULD NEVER DELEGATE . . .

- A shift in priorities without a simultaneous shift in resource allocation is delusional. Anytime we announce new initiatives or change priorities, it requires a change in how we are allocating our resources (team, time, and money). It also requires that we do less of one thing to allow us to do more of something else. None of us has the ability to keep adding without curtailing or stopping something else.
- Business success is highly dependent on who you hire and who you don't fire.
- Motivation is for amateurs. Pros never need motivating.
- Show me a lousy culture and I will show you a lousy CEO.
- The key is the clarity on the obstacle and consistency of disciplined execution on the critical drivers. Consistency requires measurement. Discipline requires standards. Execution requires resources.

A CRISIS IS A TERRIBLE THING TO WASTE

- The best time to learn the lessons (and avoid the dreaded dumb tax) is prior to making the mistake in the first place.
- Making mistakes is inevitable; admitting them and learning the lesson is optional. I love what Dr. Buckminster Fuller said about this: "A mistake is not a sin unless it is not admitted."
- The tougher the times, the better the people you need. There is no way to survive a bad market with weak people.
- Paying for overhead we don't need to support revenue we don't have is stupid.

ORDINARY THINGS, CONSISTENTLY DONE, PRODUCE EXTRAORDINARY RESULTS!

- Ordinary things, consistently done, produce extraordinary results! Think about the discipline of consistently reviewing your prior month's financial statements by the 10th of every month. In a matter of a quarter or two, the insights and optics harvested will change the priorities and decision making in your business.

O BABY!

- Start with what customers want. Start with their needs, desires, and pain. Start with the gap between the solutions being offered by the competition and where they (the customers) are frustrated.

HELP ME UNDERSTAND

- When my effort to help you get better exceeds your effort to get better, this stops working for both of us.
- In dealing with employees, I have found one universal truth: They all want to be successful. The key is alignment on definitions of success.
- The clearer we are on the coaching of *beliefs* and performance by shifting the burden of ownership and correction to the employee, the less the likelihood we will have to resort to begging, threats, and consequences.
- The only difference between a high-maintenance and a high-performance team is a culture of accountability, measuring, and ownership.

OPPORTUNITY WITHOUT STRUCTURE IS . . .

- Opportunity without structure is chaos.

- No leverage, no long-term growth. The inevitable result is chaos and a gravitational pull toward the urgent. Leverage is the bridge that transitions the Owner of a business from Operator mode to Owner mode.

- The price of entrepreneurial success is discipline and structure.

MANN GULCH

- When the environment radically changes and you are confronted with moments of uncertainty and danger, clinging to the old "right" way might seem like a good idea, but it can frequently be deadly.

- New circumstances always require new skills and tools, fresh training, innovative solutions, superior team members. The alternative (relying on past answers) is often a prescription for suffering and failure to survive.

- Sometimes the problem we started out to solve mutates. If we miss the shift, we will try to solve the new problem using solutions for the old problem. Chances are, those old solutions for the previous problem are useless.

DREAMS AND DEMAND

- When it comes to goals, far too much emphasis is placed on visualizing Oz and not enough on designing and constructing the yellow brick road. Goals are not plans. Goals are ideas, and few things are dumber than executing on an idea with no plan or planning.

- About the stupidest thing management can do is to announce some lofty goal for the year ("Our revenue target is $6,000,000 this year.") without any thought about the working plan to attain it.

- One of the hardest parts of designing the journey is being sober about reality and painstakingly honest about your current situation. Psychiatric hospitals are filled with people who are delusional about reality.

- My life works to the degree I keep my commitments.

- Don't let your obsession with the dream get in the way of noticing the demand. Or as my friends on Wall Street say, "When the duck quacks, feed it."

THE BIG 8

- Leaders inspire . . . Managers control. To be successful in business, we need both.

- Without a dashboard, you get a story. Dashboards tell you what you need to know, not what you want to believe.

- Without coaching and consequences, good intentions and "the best I can" will become the excuse du jour. Without coaching and consequences, critical drivers and outcomes will become suggestions, not standards.

- If they [your employees] create it [the plan], they own it.

- You cannot babysit your way to high performance and accountability.

- Information is simply data that has been organized, which is the role of a dashboard. I need knowledge, not more information.

SOMETHING FOR NOTHING . . . SERIOUSLY?

- Never buy anything from someone who is out of breath.

- Passive anything is a bad idea and ultimately unworkable because it requires us to fall into the trap of thinking there is a way to do nothing and still get what we want or to maintain what we have by being inactive. No part of your life or business works that way.

THE ONLY CONSTANT IN BUSINESS IS . . .

- The only constant in business is change.

- The reason companies lose relevance, go broke, or fade into the sunset is because they continue to grow, but fail to evolve. They rely on the wrong questions and old answers. Great questions, an open mind, flexibility, and a healthy dose of paranoia are your best friends in business. No business is safe: 435 of the Fortune 500 (87%) from 1955 are now gone . . . disappeared . . . kaput. The business environment kept on changing—requiring a different set of answers—and they didn't come up with a better question. Stupid!

EVERYTHING COUNTS

- When I see this kind of poor performance on a consistent basis, it can only be a result of one of four things:
  - Incompetent and uncaring employees (This is a hiring and culture issue.)
  - A lack of training
  - No measurements or accountability
  - A lack of supervision
- A discount for future services as compensation for poor performance on past services is analogous to getting salmonella at a restaurant and the restaurant owner offering me a free dessert the next time I eat there. I already got sick from this ill-conceived trip, and your idea of helping me get over the food poisoning is to offer a token discount on my next trip?

THE 3 PILLARS OF SUCCESS

- We make promises to ourselves, but we break them with alarming regularity. For some reason, promises we make to ourselves are less sacred than the promises we make to others. Having an accountability partner who will hold you to your commitments is a key ingredient to making sustainable progress and for success. Someone

who will tell you the truth; someone who will not buy into your
cheap excuses for why you fell off the wagon or didn't get the job
done; someone to tell you "no."

- The higher you go or the better you want to get, the greater the
  requirement to have someone in your life who will hold you
  accountable and tell you the truth.

THE ADVANTAGE OF BEING SMALL

- The only things "small" has going for it are flexibility and intimacy
  of relationships.

- Survival requires more curiosity and less arrogance; more humility
  and less need to be right; better questions and fewer answers.

SIMPLIFYING GROWTH

- The reason we gravitate to a tactical answer is because we are
  hardwired to get busy . . . to do something . . . to take action. The
  illusion we live with is that being active is synonymous with being
  productive. Dumb!

- Who do I want to buy from me?

- What must happen to cause them to buy?

- What must happen to keep them coming back?

- What could happen to cause them not to buy?

THE BATHROBE THEORY OF BUSINESS: WHEN A GOOD IDEA ISN'T

- In our desire for certainty, a map, and familiar landmarks, we tend
  to look for patterns that will tell us a story and provide an illusion of
  safety. An inability or unwillingness to distinguish between the story
  and the facts, however, has caused more than a few bankruptcies.

- Business is not a bathrobe. One size does not fit all. Different problems in different environments for different people at different stages of development require different solutions. Never ask an encyclopedia salesman if you need an encyclopedia. He has the kind of one-size-fits-all mentality that will wreck your business.

YOU, INC.

- You cannot have financial freedom without financial discipline.

- Every rich person I know has a job to do at the company they work for. And every one of these successful people "owns" their job. Sometimes the job they own is for a company they own and sometimes the job they own is for a business controlled by others. Either way, they have taken ownership of their work—the work performed and the outcomes produced. The job, like everything else in their life, is an extension of their identity and the narrative they have created about who they are and how they will perform their work.

- Great business owners aren't born with business knowledge. The successful ones studied, practiced, and mastered the art and science of business leadership, leverage, planning, and measurement. If you happen to have "business Owner" as one of the jobs you need to perform, you will need to learn the skills of business ownership in addition to the skills of your profession.

- If YOU, Inc. were a publicly held company with stockholders, would your stock price be rising, falling, or treading water?

KEEPING THE LUG NUTS TIGHT

- Systems are wonderful for creating consistency but rarely result in excellence.

- Keeping the lug nuts tight is a cultural issue, not a systems problem. A culture that loses focus on training, has an unwillingness to measure, and has an aversion to holding people accountable will always result in lost productivity and loose lug nuts.

THE APOLOGY

- If the culture in your business is to change, then it will start with you apologizing to your employees.

HOW AM I GOING TO PLAY THE SECOND HALF?

- The key to mastering the art of living starts with defining your vision of excellence!

- There is a big difference between success and excellence. Success is getting there. Excellence is staying there.

EXECUTION

- The success of all strategies ultimately depends on execution. You can have the greatest strategy in the world, but if the strategy is not consistently executed, it will fail. The obvious corollary is that a poor strategy perfectly executed will also fail.

- Time is the enemy of choices. The shorter the time, the fewer the choices.

- Start where you are. Don't let perfect get in the way of possible. Or as my dad used to tell me, "Shiny shoes don't help you walk any faster." I'll say this a different way: the goal is not to get the anchor all the way back into the boat. To make forward progress, we only need to get it a quarter of an inch off the bottom.

- A good idea for you could be a bad idea for me. It depends on our respective ability, resources, and willingness to consistently execute.

STRATEGIC GROWTH

- Understanding Point A and Point B gives you clarity about the gap you are dealing with. Clarifying the gap is critical because residing in this gap is the obstacle that is preventing forward progress from here to there. All obstacles are in the gap between where you are and where you want to be. If you cannot identify a gap, the obstacle isn't even on your radar.

- You can't create a strategy or prioritize your resources until you have clarity on the opportunity and the obstacles preventing progress toward the attainment of that opportunity (outcome).

- A strategy is the *idea* about what needs to happen to overcome the obstacle preventing forward progress. Without clarity about the core problem (the obstacle), a plan (the specific action steps required to implement the strategy) is a waste of time.

- This "buy a bigger bullhorn, find a taller mountain, and scream it at the top of your lungs" approach is a poor substitute for a razor-sharp focus on market segments and on discovering the true pain/problem your product or service solves.

- We want to minimize the brain damage of becoming a "me too" business with no meaningful competitive promise and, therefore, an inability to articulate a valid reason for the customer to make the switch from a competitor to you. I will remind you that differentiation is not a promise.

- You are running two businesses simultaneously: the one that is providing revenue today and the one that will generate revenue tomorrow. It is highly unlikely they are the same business.

- Sustained success requires strategy. And strategy requires
  - clarity on the obstacle or problem;
  - a plan to overcome the obstacle;
  - a structure for the allocation of resources;
  - prioritization of time and activities; and
  - an analysis of risk.

  Marketing is about getting people to notice what you do. Execution is about doing something people will notice. Never assume it is all one and none of the other. Strategic growth requires both!

SYSTEMS VS. FLEXIBILITY

- Systems foster the illusion of "safe."

- When the environment changes, which it seems to be doing with ever-greater frequency and severity, the old way of doing things is a killer.

- Correlation is not causation. God is love. Love is blind. Ray Charles is blind . . . but that doesn't make Ray Charles God.

- Systems are great at draining an organization of passion and flexibility. Use them carefully or you will pay a very heavy dumb tax. Besides, how can you deliver exceptional service if you are unwilling to make exceptions? Who do you know that doesn't want to be the exception to all the stupid rules and policies we are forced to deal with on a daily basis? I rest my case.

CORRECTING THE BUSINESS MODEL

- I suspect you are like me and most other business owners I know who have decided to grow our businesses in an attempt to become more successful. And, like me, you have occasionally experienced less profitability and cash flow as a result of that flurry of activity. Outgrowing your business model is usually visible when your machine starts to rattle or inefficiencies pop up, resulting in smaller bottom line profits and more drama. That's a sure sign you have a business model problem, not a marketing challenge.

INDIGESTION (1 + 1 ≠ 2)

- Hand-crank businesses (low leverage, no machine) consume resources and are difficult to profitably scale.

- Everything requires maintenance to avoid decomposition and decay.

- Most businesses die of indigestion, not starvation. Pouring gasoline into a hand crank does not produce progress; it starts fires.

IF YOU WANT TO GROW . . .

- The mistake most of us make in the hope of boosting sales is to keep flogging our products to new markets using new communication and messaging tactics.

- The only way you can describe the difference between you and everybody else who wants their business is to have a granular understanding of what your competitors do and how what you do is meaningfully different. You must be able to tell a customer: "This is what we do and here is why *this* is important and unique. Other venders do not do *this*; they do *that*. If you want *that*, you should buy from them. If you want *this*, you should buy from us."

- Value created but not delivered is of no value. Value delivered but not perceived is of no value. In other words, it does no good to wink at a pretty girl with the lights out . . . you're the only one who knows what you did. If you want to get noticed, turn the lights on.

- Honing your conversion technique or initiating a social media and SEO strategy is not the same as clarity about:
  - what customers (current and potential) want;
  - what they are afraid of;
  - how they define success;
  - how we message the difference that makes the difference; and
  - what solution must be designed, promised, and delivered to exceed their expectations and meet their definition of success.

    As Peter Drucker insightfully suggested, "The customer rarely buys what the business thinks it is selling."

- Few growth strategies are more powerful than giving the customer certainty of success.

ON VS. IN

- The problem is NOT that they are in their business, however; rather, the problem is that they have not learned the critical business skills required to make the shift from "Operator" to "Owner." They haven't learned how to prioritize, allocate resources, hire, delegate, leverage, create a culture, read financial statements, create processes, build the structure, and install dashboards, accountability, and critical drivers. It's not that they don't want to; it's that no one ever taught them how.

- The moment you "disengage" from your business, you have shifted from "Owner" to "Investor," and now there needs to be someone else in the business to run things.

NOT ALL RISKS ARE CREATED EQUAL

- Not all progress is measured by ground gained. Sometimes progress is measured by losses avoided.
- The key to avoiding losses is minimizing risk. The prerequisite to minimizing risk is identifying and understanding it in all its forms.
- When you think about what could go wrong, you dramatically increase the odds of creating something that will go right.

THE TRIANGLE OF DEATH

- The customer has the only vote on whether or not that promise was delivered.
- The power of designing your success proposition is that it will not only communicate to the target market your promise but also dictate the internal priorities and skill sets you must master to deliver that promise.
- It's hard to be the low-cost provider if you are not the low-cost producer! (Or, as one of my mentors told me forty years ago, "Price is only important when quality is an insufficient substitute.")
- It is rare (if not impossible) to find a business that delivers the highest quality, in the shortest period of time, at the lowest price, and has a world-class customer experience process.

- You can't be important everywhere, so be important where it counts.

MOMMAS LOVE THEIR BABIES

- You and your customers are in a relationship. Relationships tend to work best when the focus is on meeting the needs of the other party, not our own.

- You can have a crappy product and still become über successful. It's not about the product!

- Your success will have very little to do with what you do and everything to do with how you do it. Never, ever forget that.

- Instead of falling in love with our products, we would all be more successful if we fell in love with our customers and their outcomes!

PRIORITIZING GROWTH STRATEGIES

- It makes no sense to try to get more when you are not optimizing what you've already got. I'll repeat that: It. Makes. No. Sense.

- The genius of a great business is a maniacal focus on the customer and his outcomes, frustrations, and success.

- Sustainable growth requires two things: keeping the customers you've got, and adding new ones.

- Mastery = Practicing the right thing in an effort to get better. When the training stops, so does the progress. Candidly, I have found that I am not talented or smart enough to be unprepared.

- Increasing revenue and sabotaging profits is a formula for poor.

- Optimize before you maximize.

- Getting big is the result of success. Success is not the result of getting big. One of your jobs is to carefully consider the various strategies available to you for growing your business. Lurching for the "more leads" lever is rarely the best or most effective alternative.

- Developing a strategy to grow revenue is important, but growing revenue without growing profits and cash flow is dumb. Successful businesses have figured out how to do both.

CREATING ENTERPRISE VALUE

- A business that is exitable at the highest possible value has an Owner that obsessed about the predictability and sustainability of the future stream of earnings.
- Regardless of the decision to sell or not, the path to maximizing the enterprise value and creating exitability remains the same: Grow the earnings and control risks.
- The things that can go wrong are the things that jeopardize the enterprise value and exitability.
- Do not confuse sustainability with stability. Volatility is not synonymous with risk.
- Regardless of your firefighting expertise, knowing where the gasoline is stored prior to the fire is critical to preventing the building from exploding in the event of an ill-conceived match.
- Minimizing the internal and external risks and how these risks impact the predictability and sustainability of your future stream of earning is critical to the value of your business and your ultimate exitability as an Owner.

IT'S NOT ABOUT THE PLAN

- The value of planning is the clarity of being able to explain your strategy and blueprint to increase your level of financial success in the current environment, which is very different from being able to explain how the current environment has impacted your level of financial success. One is planning and the other is a justification.
- You are executing on an idea if there is no plan, which never ends well. A flurry of tactical activities to move the needle is the formula for drama and chaos.

- If you cannot get clarity on the plan to achieve the outcome, change the outcome. Even with a plan, you probably will not hit the bull's-eye, but at least you will not end up in a graveyard.

MY BIGGEST PROBLEM IS . . .

- Everyone wants to go to heaven, no one wants to die. There is no success without sacrifice.
- Being addicted to learning is critical to success . . . but so is being addicted to the business end of a shovel. Problems deferred are problems magnified.

OPTIONS ANALYSIS MATRIX

- All choices require a trade-off and sacrifice. You can have almost anything you want . . . you just can't have everything you want.
- The key to successful options analysis is to actually see your choices in a comparative format. Trying to weigh the pros and cons of each choice in your head is a fool's game that inevitably leads to a dumb (inferior) choice.

CAUSE AND EFFECT

- Whenever the effect is missing, so is the cause. Execute and manage the cause and the effect will take care of itself.
- The hard part is not envisioning the outcome or setting the goal. It's figuring out what needs to change and consistently executed to reach this outcome. If you know what needs to change and get executed, you know what needs to be measured. These are your critical drivers. Execute on the critical drivers and close the gap.

WHAT GETS MEASURED IS . . .

- What gets measured is what gets done. What gets measured is what gets managed. What gets measured and reported can improve exponentially.

THE GREAT QUESTION

- All activities consume resources. You can't shift priorities without simultaneously shifting resources.

- We tend to default into thinking that lots of things are important and that narrowing our priorities down to just a few is impossible or unrealistic, given all the stuff that needs attention. Let me assure you it's not. My rule is: Start fewer things, finish more things.

- The great question is: "What am I optimizing for? In other words, what is the one major that, if accomplished, would have the most significant impact on my business?"

ADVICE FROM THE CHAIRMAN OF THE BOARD

- It turns out that the key to getting rich is to avoid doing stupid things. The vast majority of dumb tax in both of our lives is a direct result of emotional and optimistic decisions.

- Operators react and sweat. Owners think and plan.

- If the Owner of the team made his decisions by first sitting through a pep rally from a motivational coach, we would have a very enthusiastic Owner with no money. No exceptions. Owners and members of a Board of Directors do not work themselves into an emotional frenzy prior to a Board meeting. Ever!

- Skepticism and thinking are your best friends when sitting in the Owner's box.

- Every business is just one bad decision away from a financial disaster.

- Doubling the horsepower of the engine in your car or substituting rocket fuel for your unleaded gas will not enable the car to go two times faster. Scaling mediocrity produces bigger piles of mediocrity, not success. Always optimize first.

- Growth is what you say "yes" to. Success is what you say "no" to. The hardest thing in business is figuring out what to say "no" to. Warren Buffett said it best: "The difference between successful people and very successful people is that very successful people say no to almost everything."

- Scaling a hand-crank process does not result in more bottom line profits. It results in more "crankers."

- The first step in self-delusion is denial. Where are we running with scissors?

- Risks and facts don't cease to exist just because I ignore them, and thinking that risk is under control is the greatest risk there is.

- As CEO, your job is to carefully and selectively prioritize the few key strategies and initiatives that will optimize the financial performance of the business while simultaneously leveraging the resources available. Prioritize the things that aren't in place but, if they were, would make the biggest difference to the business.

- Courage is a key ingredient for leadership. In fact, every failure of leadership has at its root a lack of courage.

- A Board of Directors knows that a plan that requires you to dodge all the bullets to be successful is not a plan; it's a hallucination.

- Business is an intellectual sport. We make the mistake of believing we can somehow get rich or become successful by
  - being passionate enough;
  - wanting it desperately enough;
  - visualizing it long enough;

- believing that we are entitled enough;

- being talented enough; and/or

- working hard enough.

  It doesn't work that way. Passion and desire might produce a willingness to persist, but they do not teach the skills and tools to create the success. The advice (and book) *Do What You Love, The Money Will Follow* is as stupid as it is destructive. This is analogous to saying, "Eat What You Want and Be Skinny."

- Investing is about the future, and the future is unknown (by everyone). Believing with all your heart, staring in the mirror, telling yourself how special you are, and mustering all the certainty you can access that the future is a sure thing do not cause it to be so . . . ever. Do not make the mistake of confusing certainty with clarity; they are two different things!

- Here is the real "secret": The chance of success goes up when you think, plan, consistently execute the right things, and worry about the possibility of loss.

ONE LAST THING

- Pleasure is about stimulating the senses. Happiness is found by being grateful for what I've got. Success is getting what I want. Fulfillment is giving what I've got.

INVITATION TO A
BOARD OF DIRECTORS

KEYS TO THE VAULT®

The following is a sample invitation sent to business owners and CEOs to join our Board of Directors.

Making the critical decision to work on the business end of your business for the next year, to really dig into your business and think about where and how you want to drive it going forward, is significant. Having me and a group of smart people support you in your thinking/planning process so that you can get better optics, question assumptions, create robust choices, make great decisions, avoid the "dumb tax," execute consistently, and have the accountability required to make sustainable progress will result in significant insights, solutions, stabilization, and growth.

OUTCOMES AND BENEFITS

Here is the truth: If you want to go somewhere you have never been, it is a great idea to have a guide. "Pin the Tail on the Donkey" (trial and error) is a stupid way to try to become successful at anything.

Think about the following: What costs me money is "What Don't I See?" What none of us can see are our assumptions about our "good" ideas. We tend to be astonishingly optimistic in our thinking and plans. The initial optimism and subsequent problems are closely linked. The culprit is not having enough wise voices in the conversation.

When I look at the majority of my problems, the common denominator was having only one voice in my head when the decision was made . . . *mine*. The truth is, adding additional voices to the conversation (advice, counsel, best practices, tough questions, optics, insights, and wisdom from other smart people) is mandatory if we expect to achieve our full potential and maximize our results. Without the advice and additional voices, we commit the most fatal of mistakes—going the wrong direction enthusiastically.

We both have had the experience of getting stuck, being confused and uncertain about which decision must be made or what direction to take to best optimize our results. One of the outcomes of a Board is to provide clarity and act as a sounding board for its members. Too many entrepreneurs and business owners rely on the formula of "My Idea + My Experience." Unfortunately, this formula is a prescription for disaster. Everyone needs the benefit of fresh insights and the best practices of other business people who bring new perspectives and ideas to our problems.

A sustainably successful business requires an additional set of discriminating eyes to help identify the risks and 2nd-order consequences of our decisions and plans. We need optics and insights to identify areas where we could be structured differently or restructured and streamlined so we can grow and optimize our results. My view is that all of us need as many ideas as possible about the challenges we are facing. In fact, my experience is this: The best way to have a great idea is to have a lot of ideas and then to pick the best one. I intend to contribute to both.

As you may or may not know, I have extensive and significant experience in doing this kind of work, most of which involves $3 million to $150 million/year businesses. I have been the CEO and/or founder as well as the hired-gun turnaround expert for numerous (>20) businesses in multiple industries, so I am confident about the impact I will have on your business decisions.

One of the major keys to my success has been to surround myself with advisors who not only watch for obstacles, icebergs, detours, or looming problems but also tell me the truth and hold me accountable. Making plans and annual budgets is one thing, but the best business owners in the world are fanatics at measuring and accountability. If you don't want to measure, you don't want to be held accountable.

One of the problems we all have in business is that since we created the machine we currently have, it is often difficult for us to see how to tweak or rebuild or reinvent our machine without the help of an outsider's perspective so that we can produce superior results. Further, environmental changes (the economy, competition, consumer preferences, regulations, etc.) can create states of disequilibrium that require an outside perspective to identify root problems/solutions that are virtually impossible for the Creator to see. Finally, every business has slippage, meaning that over time things just kind of evolve. One day you wake up and look at what you have created and decide this isn't exactly what you intended, so a change is required.

All business owners and entrepreneurs have a common problem: how to build a qualified group of advisors who will help counsel, watch, direct, set strategic direction, monitor execution, and progress toward the objectives and goals of the business as well as generate new ideas to build, grow, market, expand, and diversify their businesses. What most entrepreneurs end up with is either no advisors or a couple of local, well-known successful businesspeople who, if you're lucky, agree to attend a couple of meetings per year to approve the minutes from the last meeting, the annual budgets, the new bank financing, the stock option plan, the officers' annual compensation plan, and then adjourn, eat lunch, and play some golf. Not exactly what I need when I'm trying to run and optimize my businesses.

Participating in a peer group setting and working on other people's business problems is a great way to get clear on issues and ideas that will support you and your business. Our Board of Directors *is designed to be your business advisors. I believe the most powerful business decision I ever made was to intentionally work with a peer group for advice, optics, and accountability.*

PROCESS

At each Board meeting, each member (15 people/Board) will have an opportunity to present his or her business and its situation, opportunities, issues, and problems. Your Board, acting in an advisory capacity, will help you identify, evaluate, and resolve outstanding issues and problems, generate new ideas and solutions, avoid doing something stupid (the dreaded dumb tax), as well as hold you accountable for your plan as the year progresses. I will act as the moderator and Chairman for these discussions as well as be an active participant in all the discussions.

Your Board will evaluate your numbers, your business plans, your marketing, your niche, and your team as well as help you identify new markets and growth opportunities. Nothing with respect to your business and its success will be off-limits. We will advise you on what we see that might be obstacles to your future growth and how you could significantly accelerate your progress and profits. We will ask you tough questions and get you to look at the most fundamental issues of your business.

A WORD OF CAUTION

Obviously, this type of meeting is designed for people who are interested in dramatically increasing the size and efficiency of their business while simultaneously avoiding disaster. People who are not yet in business, need massive psychological counseling, are trying to figure out what to do with their life, or are interested in being "passive" are not candidates for the Board. This is not a seminar but rather a working business meeting in which we facilitate the discussion, growth, and sustainable optimization of each member's business.

You will be expected to take your participation *very* seriously. You will be expected to prepare and circulate an agenda and progress report for each meeting just like you would for any other critical business meeting. You will be expected to contribute to each of your fellow members' discussions and to be active and thought-provoking in your participation. You will be expected to call it tight and say what needs to be said. I repeat: This is not a seminar. It is a business meeting at the highest level, so do not expect to be passive, to be spoon-fed, or to attend unprepared.

The Board of Directors is not for the faint of heart, the "toe dippers," or the undecided. If you know you require highly discriminating advice and counsel on an extremely personal and customized basis; if you want to dramatically grow your business and develop new strategies and execution techniques; if you know there are solutions to your problems but you don't know which one is the best track for you and your business; if you need to generate new ideas and strategies; and if you know that being held accountable is THE key to your success; then the Board of Directors is the perfect opportunity!

I know of no better way to maximize and optimize the financial results of your business than to surround yourself with a Board who will ask that you step up and play at the highest level for one year.

Thank you again for your commitment to yourself and your growth and for your trust and confidence in me! I have been through this process numerous times with other people, so you will be in very good hands.

I look forward to working with you at the highest level.

Best,

KJC

Keith J. Cunningham
Keith@KeystotheVault.com

CEO SCORECARD®

The following is a sample scorecard I have implemented for the CEOs, Pres-idents, or General Managers of the businesses I own. Whether you are the Owner and CEO of a business or an Owner with a senior leadership team, the following template will support you in designing the scorecard so that everyone knows exactly what must happen to earn an A and win this game. The beauty of this kind of specificity and clarity is the opportunity it provides to coach performance and identify needed corrections.

SCORECARD FOR CHIEF EXECUTIVE OFFICER

Create and lead our business so we are the "employer of choice" while maintaining the desired profitability targets. We are a company who puts employees before customers. Employees are acknowledged and appre-ciated. Customers are served and appreciated . . . and they consistently appreciate and acknowledge our commitment to excellence. We set stan-dards, measure critical drivers, hold each other accountable, and have candid conversations. In all matters, we have three basic rules:

1. Do the right thing.

2. Do the best we can.

3. Show others that we care.

OUTCOMES

1. **Financial**
   a. Attain Gross Revenue of:
   b. $ _____ by December 2017 (1 year)
   c. $ _____ by December 2019 (3 years)
   d. $ _____ by December 2021 (5 years)
   e. Attain _____ % Gross Margin by December 2017.
   f. Attain _____ % EBITDA by December 2017.
   g. Attain _____ % of Cash Flow from Operations by December 2017.
   h. A/R below _____ days in 2017
   i. Debt reduction of at least $_____ in 2017

2. **Create and maintain a company that is proud of and protects its culture** of respect, integrity, intelligence, and productivity: a culture that is based on trust, appreciation, candor, excellence, and improvement.
   a. Customer Satisfaction is at least 4.5 out of 5 by December 2017.
   b. Employee Satisfaction is at least 4.0 out of 5 by December 2017.
   c. Every employee receives at least quarterly coaching on their specific results.
   d. All employees above XXX level use the monthly or weekly "Managing by Objectives," or "MBO," process.
   e. Net Promoter Score "NPS" is 75% by December 2017.
   f. Employee turnover (they quit) is <5% in 2017.
   g. We should never be surprised when an employee quits and they should never be surprised when their employment is terminated.

3. **Create and maintain an outcomes-based organization filled with A players** who are self-driven and want to be held accountable and rewarded for achieving outcomes and results. Comprised of people with a high internal emotional need to succeed, a commitment to growth, and a desire to improve.

   a. 85% of all personnel are true A players, as measured by their performance against their standards and their cultural fit.

   b. 15% are B players being coached/trained into A players and have a specific, personalized path to attain A-player status.

   c. 0% C/D players

   d. A specific onboarding plan for every new hire, regardless of the position

   e. 100% of personnel have and maintain a scorecard.

   f. 100% of personnel have a dashboard that monitors performance of critical drivers.

   g. 100% of personnel have compensation packages that include base salary and personal performance bonuses.

   h. 100% of raises, bonuses, commissions, and promotions are based upon attainment of outcomes, results, and standards.

   i. 100% of all hiring selections and promotions are evaluated and selected using the Topgrading process. (You must read *Who* by Geoff Smart for more about this interviewing and hiring methodology.)

4. **Create and maintain an organization committed to excellence and growth** by providing opportunities for learning and training to improve the skills of their current position, begin learning skills for advancement or cross training, and improve each person's overall mental wellness.

   a. All employees receive monthly or quarterly training of at least 5 hours per quarter; 20 hours per year is the minimum. Training can be either internal or external . . . either job-specific or general improvement. More is better.

   b. All employees are to "read" at least one assigned book per quarter . . . to be discussed at one of the training meetings.

    c. All employees' specific work and processes are documented so that a new person could take over this position and know what to do or where to look to learn how to do it.

    d. All employees are trained to backfill another position in the event of a sudden loss of an employee. Redundancy of expertise is critical when we do not have the money for bench strength. This level of redundancy would keep us out of the emergency room and functioning, but it does not need to be designed to perfection or permanence. Duct tape is good until a permanent solution is found.

COMPETENCIES: THE SKILLS AND BEHAVIORS REQUIRED FOR THE JOB

Focus the company on outcomes and results.

Establish clear and concise outcomes for the company and maintain an outcomes-based organization chart. Establish clear links between the company's outcomes and an individual's outcomes and results. Make sure each employee understands how they contribute to the company's mission, outcomes, and results. Ensure that each leader, manager, and staff member has an outcomes-based scorecard that maps to the company's outcomes and results. Plan and run meetings based on outcomes and results. Help design briefings, reports, agendas, and meeting materials that are focused on outcomes and results. Avoid allocating time to discussions of subjects such as activities, busyness, or hours worked.

Be strategic in your thinking and tactical in your actions.

Being clear on the problem, obstacle, or gap to be bridged is critical, since solving the problem that isn't is a waste of time and resources (and, to be candid, irritates me). Developing a specific plan to overcome this obstacle is critical; otherwise, we run the risk of running the wrong direction enthusiastically. Finally, being tactical in your actions puts rubber on the road and facilitates forward progress.

Always be willing to ask the question "What can I do today to improve our situation?"

Do not let perfect get in the way of possible. You might not have the final answer, but you can find two or three things to do to improve our current position. When in doubt, do these two or three things.

Preserve relationships.

It really is a small world, and what comes around goes around.

Be good at being **both** *kind* **and** *driven.*

Address everyone with kindness and consideration regardless of the topic at hand, even if the topic is missed expectations or poor performance. Demonstrate the ability to remain focused on outcomes and results while doing so in a manner that is attractive to our leaders, managers, and staff. Run and participate in meetings in a manner that elicits input from everyone. React to input and ideas in a way that makes people glad they spoke up and leads them to speak again. Make it clear to everyone around you that you actively desire input, new ideas, and feedback and that it will be used to actually make the company better.

Be a master at delegation, and do not abdicate your leadership.

Be efficient and effective by delegating an outcome or result rather than an activity or a task. Ensure that the person clearly understands the outcome and the time frame in which the result is expected. Determine if the person responsible for delivering an outcome understands how to produce the result by working closely with them to develop their achievement plan. Provide coaching or training if needed and conduct periodic progress sessions. Stay close to the delegated task and remain part of the success of its achievement. Work with the person so they understand and accept the reasoning behind the delegated outcome and why they received it. It is important that they understand this even if they disagree with being the recipient of the delegated outcome.

Be physically present and involved.

Get out of your office and spend face time with our staff. Get out of your office and spend face time physically with our customers. Customers pay us the money and employees do the work, so in reality there are very few reasons for you to be sitting behind your desk. We are in a people business, and our people and customers like the personal touch of the CEO caring enough to spend time with them. This matters, this is important, and this is not something you do when you find some time. Make it a scheduled, embedded part of your calendar.

Attract, hire, develop, and retain only A players.

Build our organization with A players. Demonstrate that you have proven ways to identify A-player talent and that you can teach this skill to other leaders. Demonstrate the ability to hire these A players into our company and how you can help them develop both personally and professionally. Show that you know how to retain this level of talent within our organization.

Thrive in a competitive market.

Understand the competition as well as the marketplace (environment). Both change frequently. Understand our customers' pains to avoid and gains to get criteria and how our business intersects with these vectors. Understand and proactively act on the risks, friction points, differences that make the difference, and success proposition criteria of both our existing customers as well as our marketplace.

Think.

Spend at least ___ hours per week in Thinking Time sessions with a high-quality question. While some of these questions will be tactical, the majority should be strategic and be based on bottlenecks, gaps in performance, leverage, underutilized assets, priorities, direction, and asset allocation.

Be successful and comfortable in a small business.

Be comfortable acting on the old motto "No challenge is too large and yet no task is too small." Be comfortable working in a small, tight-knit family of people all carrying multiple, simultaneous responsibilities. Demonstrate your understanding of the fact that you need these people far more than they need you.

Make us better by learning lessons.

Make the company better with each event. We have the ability to learn from each success and failure. When an A player joins us, let's learn why, and when an A player leaves, let's learn why they made this decision. When a strategy works, let's learn why; and when strategies fail, let's figure out what went wrong and how we can avoid this mistake in the future. Create and oversee a company improvement initiative with expected results and actions as well as periodic follow-ups.

Leave your ego out.

Your success will not be based on being right, righteous, or smart. Your success is measured by producing results, regardless of the source of the idea that produced them. Be humble and give the team the credit. After all, you are merely pointing the flashlight; they are doing all the digging.

Be intelligent.

Learn fast and demonstrate the ability to quickly and proficiently understand and absorb new information. Be able to structure and process qualitative or quantitative data and draw insightful conclusions from it.

Focus on your outcomes and results—produce.

Clearly understand the outcomes and standards expected of you and your position. Commit to your outcomes, establish clear work plans (MBOs) to achieve each outcome, and measure yourself as well as your team. Know at all times if you are meeting your commitments, attaining your outcomes, and producing the value expected of you. Get and stay organized. Get and stay focused on your outcomes. Prioritize and operate with a major objective as the goal line. Be proactive and pay attention to detail. Avoid interesting activities (shiny pennies) that distract you from your outcomes.

Be flexible and adaptable.

_____ is a small business that is growing fast and expanding into new markets. Outcomes, standards, responsibilities, approaches, methodologies, and strategies will change from time to time—sometimes with your consent and approval; sometimes without. Be able to adjust quickly to changing priorities and conditions and be able to cope effectively with complexity and change.

Always invest in learning, growing, and improving yourself.

Never be good enough. Never be smart enough. Never know all there is to know about leading, attracting new business, servicing our customers, or building the team. Demonstrate a continuous desire to learn by reading books (I read two to three per week), watching videos, attending seminars, and going to formal training. Be willing to spend your own money and your personal time in addition to the company's. Demonstrate that you are participating in your own development, your own success, and your own growth. Visibly bring back what you learn to the company and teach others. Help others grow with you.

KEYS TO THE VAULT®
BUSINESS SCHOOL

Opportunities to Study with Keith

I have spent my business career

- mastering the critical business drivers and levers, and
- learning, practicing, and refining the distinctions and lessons that make the difference.

These drivers, levers, and distinctions serve as the foundation for all my teaching and writing and the curriculum for the Keys to the Vault® Business School.

I have distilled the past forty-plus years of successes and mistakes down to the key business strategies. The curriculum I have created and teach in the Keys to the Vault® Business School includes different programs, courses, and skills that are all designed to help you accelerate your learning as well as your financial performance and success.

- **4-Day MBA®:** A four-day classroom course in which I answer the most frequent question I'm asked when I travel around the world speaking and teaching on business: "Keith, how do I grow my business and make more money?" Regardless of where I speak, business owners tell me they feel like they have a job, not a business. They feel like their business is running them, when they should be running their business. In the 4-Day MBA® you will learn the most critical skills and tools required to run the business end of your business, the skills to grow from "Operator" to "Owner," and how to convert your "job" into a business that has lasting value. A critical part of Owner skills is financial literacy and mastering the fundamentals of financial statements, financial statement analysis, and business optics. At the end of the second day, I will hand out the financial statements of a disguised Fortune 100 company and, by looking only at the numbers, you will be able to decide if you do or don't want to own the stock. And you'll be right. The last two days are exclusively focused on growth and transitioning from Operator to Owner.

- **How to Buy (or Exit) a Business®:** A four-day classroom program that is exceptionally powerful. Many people would like to own a business but want to avoid the hard work, uncertainty, and risk associated with a start-up. Many existing business owners would like to expand via acquisition, (it is usually easier and less expensive to buy a customer than it is to win them over). Knowing how to find good companies for sale, how to locate and work with a broker, what specific questions to ask the seller and how to earn the seller's confidence, how to evaluate, how to perform the due diligence, how to value the business, how to raise the money, and how to structure the deal and calculate the purchase price are all included. Students receive a comprehensive how-to reference manual in addition to working on real-life examples in the classroom. Creating a valuable business that you can exit is the flip side of buying a business. The four critical business strategies you learn at How to Buy (or Exit) a Business are:
  - Optimizing your exitability.
  - Maximizing your exit value.

- Growth by acquisition.
- Acquisition/selling skills and tool belt.

- **Plan or Get Slaughtered®:** A two-day classroom program that focuses exclusively on successfully driving sustainable revenue. Most business owners have had the experience of hitting an invisible ceiling on top-line growth. You have a goal of increasing revenue by 10% or 25% or 50%, but you don't have an actual plan to produce the desired growth. This course teaches the strategic and tactical growth strategies required to achieve this growth and gives you actual classroom time to do the critical thinking to create that plan.

- **Board of Directors:** If you want to go to somewhere you have never been, it is a great idea to have a guide. As business owners, we tend to be astonishingly optimistic in our thinking and planning. We rarely question our assumptions, nor do we have experienced business advisors watching our progress or providing us with feedback. As a result, we commit the most fatal of mistakes: running in the wrong direction enthusiastically. The Board of Directors is an exclusive (by invitation only), twelve-month program in which fifteen entrepreneurs and business owners—who are actually in business, have revenue, and are "doing it"—meet with me three to four times per year for two or three days per meeting. I serve as Chairman of the Board. As a Board member, you have access to me for additional support, as needed, during the Board year. Having a Board of Directors who will advise, counsel, direct, set strategic priorities, monitor execution and accountability, review monthly and quarterly financial statements, review your annual plan, and provide optics—both opportunities and icebergs—is critical if you expect to achieve the goals of your business as well as generate new strategies to build, grow, market, expand, and diversify your company.

- **Private One-on-One Consulting:** Business owners, management teams, and entrepreneurs who require private, personal advice and consulting can customize time with me. Private consulting can range from half to full days, to monthly or quarterly sessions spread out over six to twelve months. Having access to a private advisor is an exceptionally powerful way to leverage your time and your results.

If you're done wasting time and money lurching from shiny pennies to magic bullets to fast-buck schemes; if you know there is a gap in your skills and tools; if you are committed to doing what it takes to achieve the results you desire and deserve; and if you are serious about reaching your full potential and breaking through as a business Owner, I want to encourage you to:

⚷ *Invest in yourself,* which is the key to growth.

⚷ *Learn the critical distinctions so you can create better choices,* which is the key to a better life.

⚷ *Do whatever it takes to create excellence, mastery, and contribution,* which are the keys to fulfillment.

Please contact us, either through email or our websites. If you're looking for answers, I can help.

info@KeystotheVault.com
www.KeystotheVault.com
www.CFOScoreboard.com
512-231-9944

ABOUT THE AUTHOR

American entrepreneur, international speaker, and acclaimed author, Keith J. Cunningham is regarded as one of the foremost authorities and teachers on business mastery. With more than forty-five years of business and investing experience, Keith has taught critical business skills to thousands of top executives, business owners, and entrepreneurs around the world.

In Keith's *Keys to the Vault®* Business School, he has created curriculum designed to accelerate the transition from Operator to Owner and drive sustainable financial performance and business success. Through his Board of Directors program, he serves as Chairman of the Board for businesses in a wide range of industries.

Reading *The Road Less Stupid* and adopting the discipline of Thinking Time will enable you to run your business more effectively, make more money, and dramatically increase the likelihood of keeping that money.

Keith is also the author of *Keys to the Vault: Lessons from the Pros on Raising Money and Igniting Your Business* and *The Ultimate Blueprint for an Insanely Successful Business*.

Keith is married to Sandi and they reside in Austin, Texas.